# Never Enough

## BREAKING THE SPIRIT OF POVERTY

# DAVID HOLDAWAY

Regal

A Division of Gospel Light
Ventura, California, U.S.A.

Published by Regal Books
A Division of Gospel Light
Ventura, California, U.S.A.
Printed in U.S.A.

Cover Design by Kevin Keller
Interior Design by Robert Williams
Edited by Kyle Duncan and David Webb

LIBRARY OF CONGRESS CATALOGING-IN-PUBLICATION DATA
Holdaway, David.
    Never enough / David Holdaway.
        p.    cm.
    Includes bibliographical references.
    ISBN 0-8307-2469-9
    1. Wealth—Religious aspects—Christianity.    I. Title.
    BR115.W4 H65    2000                                             99-056751
    241'.68—dc21

1   2   3   4   5   6   7   8   9   10   11   12   13   14   15   /   05   04   03   02   01   00

Rights for publishing this book in other languages are contracted by Gospel Literature International (GLINT). GLINT also provides technical help for the adaptation, transla-tion and publishing of Bible study resources and books in scores of languages world-wide. For further information, write to GLINT at P.O. Box 4060, Ontario, CA 91761-1003, U.S.A. You may also send E-mail to Glintint@aol.com, or visit the GLINT website at www.glint.org.

# DEDICATION

*To all those who have taught me by their lives: "It is more blessed to give than to receive" (Acts 20:35).*

# CONTENTS

# ACKNOWLEDGMENTS

Thank you to my wife, Jan, whose professional help as an editor and constant encouragement have been invaluable.

My thanks also go to Sue Bailey, our church administrator and great friend, whose suggestions and support have made a significant contribution.

And to the many wonderful servants of God mentioned in this book whose lives and testimonies have touched the world through their giving, thank you.

# STANDARD OF LIVING OR QUALITY OF LIFE?

*Whoever loves money never has money enough; whoever loves wealth is never satisfied with his income. . . . I have seen a grievous evil under the sun: wealth hoarded to the harm of its owner, or wealth lost through some misfortune, so that when he has a son there is nothing left for him. Naked a man comes from his mother's womb, and as he comes, so he departs. He takes nothing from his labor that he can carry in his hand.*

ECCLESIASTES 5:10,13-15

*Contentment comes not so much from great wealth as from few wants.*

EPICTETUS, CIRCA A.D. 100

My purpose in writing this book is to try and give a biblically balanced view of God's desire to bless and prosper His people. This involves learning not only how to receive but also how to give.

As a young Christian I remember becoming very confused over what is commonly called prosperity teaching. Its detractors claim that prosperity theology takes a "name it and claim it" approach to wealth: If we desire something, particularly a material object, simply pray to God for it and, if you have enough faith, He will give it to you.

In its best light, however, prosperity teaching is about quality of life. When done biblically, it is about tapping into the abundant *spiritual* riches that God has to offer us—regardless of our checking account balance or whether we live in Calcutta or Monte Carlo.

In those early days, I listened to tapes and read books that embraced prosperity teaching, as well as other books that condemned it. Some of my closest friends took strongly opposing views on the subject. I must confess that my initial reaction was to join the opposition, my negative stance having more to do with feelings and emotions than with theological evaluation.

I have come to learn that arguments based on emotion are never resolved by logic alone. I wonder how many hold to their theological positions because they initially react against—or take a dislike to—the teaching or the teacher! After we have made our stand, it takes a work of grace for us to be open to change and admit we might have been wrong.

I eventually came to realize that my own spiritual pendulum had swung too far away from prosperity teaching. I was doing a very good job of throwing out the baby with the bathwater. So began my journey to clarify what the Bible taught and what I was to believe, trying as best I could not to be influenced by my natural bias and prejudice.

So let me say from the beginning: I believe that the Bible teaches it is the will of God to bless and prosper His people spiritually, physically, emotionally and yes, even financially and materially. Psalm 35:27 puts it like this: "The LORD . . . delights in the well-being of his servant." Does this mean that God guarantees to each of us material wealth? No. Does He guarantee that we will live in ease and comfort? No. (Just read the book of Job to verify this.)

But does He promise that He will never leave or forsake His children? Yes (see Deut. 31:6 and Heb. 13:5). Prosperity in the Kingdom has to do with a life that is submitted to the Father's will and is cradled in His loving hand.

At the cross, Jesus died so that we might have eternal life. As Jesus hung on the tree, He became a curse for us and redeemed us in order that the blessing of God might come to us by faith (see Gal. 3:13). As Christ took on the curse of sin, He broke its power over us. He not only freed us from the law but also from our bondage to sin. He has the ability to break every curse over our lives, including the curse of poverty (i.e., financial and spiritual destitution). Jesus opened up all the riches of glory for us and to us (see Phil. 4:19).

The prophet Isaiah foretold that the Messiah will be given "a portion among the great, and he will divide the spoils with the strong" (Isa. 53:12). Paul tells us the same: Believers are coheirs with Jesus Christ (see Rom. 8:17).

God wants to prosper our lives, but that does not mean that we will all become millionaires. As the title of this book suggests, we must learn that what the world has to offer us—including money, fame and power—can never be enough. We need to learn how to live in God's abundance and break free from the spirit and power of poverty. (I will talk more about this in chapter 10.) This bondage includes the tyranny of money that hinders the release of finances for the work of God and keeps us impoverished—*no matter how much we have.*

Defining what we mean by prosperity and poverty will allow us to forego a great deal of argument and strife. When I speak of poverty, I am simply talking about the condition of always being in need—a lifestyle of constant struggle filled with anxiety and fear.

The main Old Testament words that are translated as "prosper" or "prosperity" in the *King James Bible* are *tselach, shalom* and *tob. Tselach* means to advance, to succeed and to be profitable, and can be associated with the pleasure of God (see Isa. 53:10) and the protection of God (see Isa. 54:17). *Shalom* means peace, wholeness, completeness, success and health. *Tob* means good or goodness. In its fullest meaning, prosperity means no lack, having all your needs met, even to the point of having extra with which you can bless others. God promised Abraham, "I will make you into a great nation and I will bless you; I will make your name great, and you will be a blessing" (Gen. 12:2).

God's ultimate desire for us is to worship and love Him. When we do, we will live in spiritual wealth and spiritual prosperity. When we do not follow His ways, the road always leads to spiritual poverty.

Of course, we will examine the material, practical side of wealth and prosperity. God has always had a special place in His heart for the materially poor; Jesus said that the poor are blessed (see Luke 6:20). But I do not believe that God finds pleasure in seeing His children plagued by financial hardship. Just as when the Israelites were enslaved in Egypt and cried out for their God, He still hears the cries of the poor and oppressed today.

The "Never Enough Syndrome" has two debilitating faces. One face reveals a spiritual paucity and hunger for more, regardless of how much we have or own. The other is the face of material want and need, which manifests itself in financial hardship and desperation. This book will deal with both. My hope is to offer some practical helps for identifying the signs of poverty—financial and spiritual—in your own life and then moving into prosperous, Christ-centered living.

When you measure according to Kingdom values, poverty and prosperity are about your *quality of life* rather than just your standard of living. It is possible to have a very high standard of living materially and financially and at the same time have a very low quality of life.

If prosperity is only about material wealth, then the disciples and the Early Church would not have qualified. It would have been the emperor of Rome and not the apostle Paul who was prosperous. Ponder this: When Paul came to Rome to stand trial, he was a prisoner devoid of earthly wealth, while Emperor Nero lived in luxury. Yet it was Paul who knew true prosperity. God had met all his needs and would continue to do so, while the emperor's life was miserable and empty.

It is not how much we amass but how much we are able to give and bless others that determines true prosperity in our lives. Through a lifestyle of spiritual, emotional and material selflessness we will find true joy.

Jesus said, "The thief comes only to steal and kill and destroy; I have come that they may have life, and have it to the full" (John 10:10). It is not your standard of living that is the devil's target; he is out to destroy your quality of life.

A few years ago the music world mourned the death of one of its greatest stars. Freddie Mercury, lead singer of the pop group Queen, died from AIDS. Obituaries in the newspapers quoted him as saying:

> You can have everything in the world and still be the loneliest man, and that is the most bitter type of loneliness. Success has brought me world idolization and millions of pounds, but it's prevented me from having the one thing we all need, a loving ongoing relationship. I can't win. Love is like Russian roulette for me. I try to

hold back when I am attracted to someone, but I just can't control love. It runs riot. All my one-night stands are just me playing my part.[1]

Four decades earlier in 1955, another man with everything mourned the fact that he had so little to live for. In such films as *Rebel Without a Cause,* James Dean spoke to a generation of alienated youth who venerated him even after his death. "Must I always be miserable?" Dean wrote to a girlfriend. "I don't know where I am; I want to die."[2]

Six weeks before his death, Elvis Presley was asked by a newspaper reporter, "Elvis, when you started playing music, you said you wanted three things in life. You wanted to be rich, to be famous and to be happy. Elvis, are you happy?"

Elvis replied, "No, I'm as lonely as hell."

The apostle Paul said, "I have learned to be content whatever the circumstances" (Phil. 4:11). Such contentment is a learning process and is not achieved overnight. It comes by having a thankful heart and knowing the empowering presence of Jesus in our lives.

The story is told of a farmer who had lived on the same farm all his life. It was a good farm, but with the passing years, he began to tire of it. He longed for a change, for something better. As each new day passed he found a new reason for criticizing some feature of the old place. Finally, he decided to sell and listed the farm with a real estate agent who promptly prepared a sales advertisement. As one might expect, the ad emphasized all the property's advantages: ideal location, modern equipment, healthy stock, acres of fertile ground and so forth. Before placing the ad in the newspaper, the agent called the farmer and read the copy for his approval. When he had finished, the farmer cried out, "Hold everything! I've changed my mind. I'm not going to sell. I've been looking for a place like that my whole life!"

Contentment transcends physical circumstances. Paul's letter to the Philippians was to say thank-you for the gift they had sent to him in prison. The book of Philippians is full of joy and a love for Jesus. Paul told the residents of Philippi, "Rejoice in the Lord always. I will say it again: Rejoice!" (Phil. 4:4). He declared, "I can do all things through Christ who strengthens me" (Phil. 4:13, NKJV). Whatever Paul's financial circumstances, Christ's strength enabled him to trust and to triumph. Paul was more content in his prison than the emperor was in his palace.

When I first started courting my wife, Jan, I felt as if I were walking on air. I remember clearly the night of January 9, 1981. I was driving my new car on my way to Jan's home when, suddenly, another car rushed out from a side street and crashed into me. No one was hurt, so after exchanging insurance details with the other driver, I went on my way.

What was truly amazing was that I was not disturbed at all by the damage to what had been my "beloved car." A few months earlier I would have been devastated; but now it did not affect my mood at all. Why? Because I had fallen in love with someone who two years later would become my wife. I had something much better to focus my life on than a few dents in my car.

In his autobiography *Just As I Am*, Billy Graham recalls a story that he says "shows [how] true greatness is not measured by the headlines a person commands or the wealth they accumulate. It is the inner character of the person, the undergirding moral and spiritual values and commitments that are the true measure of lasting greatness." Graham writes:

Some years ago Ruth and I had a vivid illustration of this on an island in the Caribbean. One of the wealthiest men in the world had asked us to come to his lavish home for lunch. He was 75 years old, and throughout the entire meal he seemed close to tears. "I am the most miserable man in the world," he said. "Out there is my yacht. I can go anywhere I want to. I have my private plane, my helicopters. I have everything I want to make my life happy and yet I am as miserable as hell." We talked to him and prayed with him, trying to point him to Christ, who alone gives lasting meaning to life.

Then we went down the hill to a small cottage where we were staying. That afternoon the pastor of the local Baptist church came to call. He was an Englishman, and he too was 75. A widower, he spent most of his time taking care of his two invalid sisters. He reminded me of a cricket always jumping up and down, full of enthusiasm and love for Christ and others. "I don't have two pounds to my name," he said with a smile, "but I am the happiest man on this island." "Who do you think is the richer man?" I asked Ruth after he left. We both knew the answer.[3]

You may have picked up the book in your hands because there always seems to be more month than paycheck. Perhaps you literally never have enough. Despite the fact that you work hard and are a committed follower of Christ and you give (tithe) without complaint, you still struggle to make ends meet. Hopefully, the spiritual and practical tools in this book will help you break through this financial wall in the power of Christ.

Or perhaps financial needs are not so much of a struggle for you. Still, you know that something is missing. Perhaps you are experiencing soul poverty—never having enough to fill the emptiness you feel inside. You may find yourself in constant pursuit of money, power, fame, toys, entertainment. But no matter how much you own or how much fun you have, at the end of the day you never feel content or at peace.

Do either (or both) of these descriptions fit you? If so, dear friend, read on. Let us explore the heart of a precious Father who says, "In Me, there is *always* enough."

*Notes*
1. *London Daily Mail*, November 1991.
2. Joe Hyams, *James Dean: Little Boy Lost* (New York: Putnam Books).
3. Billy Graham, *Just As I Am* (San Francisco: HarperSanFrancisco, 1999).

# CHAPTER 1

# GOD OWNS EVERYTHING

*When I have any money I get rid of it as quickly as possible,*
*lest it find a way into my heart.*

JOHN WESLEY

The hall was full of excited, exuberant Christians. The organ played, sometimes leading, other times following the emotion and response of the congregation. It was quite an experience. A big-name minister had come to town and thousands had gathered to hear this anointed man of God. I sat with my four friends, intrigued and exhilarated by what was happening all around me.

I had been a Christian for several years, but such meetings had been a rare experience for me. The praise music was loud and expressive, and it was obvious that those gathered truly loved God. That night many responded to the call for salvation, and many said they were healed. But one thing early on in the meeting spoiled it for me—and something that happened at the book table after the service made it worse.

Just before the speaker came onto the platform, a member of his ministry team stood up to announce the taking of the offering. It was a long announcement. He said God was challenging many there to give £50 (about $80), some to give £40, some £30, some £20, others £10. Some, he enthused, should give more. And on it went. I was a Bible-college student in the south of England at the time and had come intending to give, but he had stopped at £10 and my offering was a little less. What was I to do? I admit now I overreacted and did not give anything and let the whole thing bug me for the rest of the service.

It seemed the appeal for money took longer than the appeal for salvation at the end of the meeting. The whole spirit and salesmanship of how the offering was taken felt so wrong and sad. I was reminded of Leonard Ravenhill's words in his classic book *Why Revival Tarries*: "Can any deny that in the Church setup the main cause of anxiety is money? Yet that which tries the modern Church most, troubled the New Testament Church least. Our accent is on paying; theirs was on praying. When we have paid, the place is taken. When they had prayed, the place was shaken."[1]

I thought, *No wonder unbelievers are sometimes put off or take offense at Christian meetings.* Afterward, my friends and I ventured over to the book table where we were encouraged to go on a Holy Land tour with the speaker and his team. The price was more than twice as much as other Holy Land trips. I thought, *Lord, how can they do this?* I did not want to become judgmental (and I have since learned of many worthwhile things that this particular ministry does), but I determined then that I would never be gullible or allow myself to be manipulated by others in my giving to God.

The devil has developed a superb public relations strategy regarding money and the Church. He has been able to polarize attitudes to extremes, breeding confusion and suspicion inside and outside the Church. One extreme says that if you become a Christian, you could end up *poor*, because the Church is only after your money.

The other extreme says that if you give to God and His Church (or a particular ministry), you will become *rich*. Proponents of this approach admonish us to let God know what we want, make a down payment in the offering basket and God will do the rest. Simply put in your order: "Name it, claim it and frame it!" Or as some have denounced it, "Blab it and grab it."

With these two extremes, the message conveyed is either that God is poor and needs your money, or that He will make you rich if only you'll give Him your cash.

It is said that the two quickest ways to upset people are to tell them how to bring up their children and what they should do with their money. This is one of the major reasons that tithing and honoring God with our finances is not taught as much as it should be. The result is financial hardship to do God's work and a famine of blessing among God's people.

Money is mentioned in the Bible more than 2,000 times. Jesus spoke about money more than He did about heaven! This is not because money is more important, but because its use is an indicator of a person's character. A wrong attitude toward money can stop a person from getting to heaven.

So what does a *right* attitude toward money entail? Let us take a look.

## UNLOCKING A RIGHT ATTITUDE ABOUT MONEY

Many years ago, well-known British evangelist Tom Rees was working on the eastern coast of England. He believed God had spoken to him about buying a property called Hildenborough Hall near Seven Oaks, south of Kent. It had been built and occupied by a titled man named Lyle—of Tate and Lyle, a major British sugar company.

Tom sold his own property but discovered a shortfall in what was required for the purchase of the new property. One morning he received a phone call from an acquaintance who said, "Tom, during the night God laid you on my heart with a very heavy burden, and I can't understand why. But I have been praying for you. Are you in any trouble?" Tom said no, but his friend persisted. "Have you any need?" he asked. Tom again said no, because he knew there was no way this man could meet the need that he had. Again his friend persisted: "Tom, is the need financial?"

Finally Tom said, "Yes."

His friend asked, "Would a loan of £10,000 help?"

Tom said, "That is exactly what I need to go ahead with what God has told me. But do you have the resources to meet it?"

"One of my relatives has died and left me a small holding," his friend replied. "I will sell it because I work on my own and don't need another business. In prospect of the sale God would have me release to you a £10,000 loan."

Tom gratefully agreed.

A few days later his friend phoned back. "Tom, the loan is off," he said.

Tom's heart sank. He said, "Thank you anyway for your prayers and consideration."

"No, you have got it wrong. The *loan* is off—now it's a gift."

"How come?" Tom asked.

"The buyers were desperate to purchase the small holding for their business interests and they offered me £10,000 over the price. God told me I was to give it to you as a gift."

"What's the company's name?" Tom asked.

His friend replied, "Tate and Lyle."

# THE EARTH IS THE LORD'S

The earth is the LORD'S, and everything in it (Ps. 24:1).

Everything belongs to Him who created everything and He can release it to us when we have been released in giving to Him. We must not forget that God took the land of the Kenites, Kenizzites, Kadmonites, Hittites, Perizzites, Amorites, Canaanites, Girgashites and Jebusites and gave it to His people as a Promised Land. God can do this for us as well because ultimately our things (cars, houses, whatever) do not belong to us but to Him. And He can give to whomever He desires.

In Job 41:11, the Lord declares, "Everything under heaven belongs to me." We are merely His appointed managers or, to use the biblical word, "stewards" of what He owns. For most of us, the house we now call "my house" was called "my house" by someone else a few years ago. And in a few years from now, someone else may call it "my house."

The same is true with land. Years from now what we call our land will be called someone else's land. We are just temporary stewards of the things that belong to God. In Haggai 2:8 God put it this way, "The silver is mine and the gold is mine." So the issue is not how much of my money and possessions will I give to God, but rather how much of God's money should I keep for myself?

Everything comes from you, and we have given you only what comes from your hand (1 Chron. 29:14).

Amy Carmichael was an Irish missionary, called as a young woman to go to India. After first traveling to Japan, then China and Sri Lanka, she finally arrived in India where she founded the Dohnavur Fellowship, a refuge for children in moral and mortal danger. She spent the next 53 years there without furlough. She said, "You can give without loving, but you cannot love without giving."[2]

Carmichael emphasized what Jesus taught as He watched what the people were putting into the Temple treasury (see Mark 12:41-44; Luke 21:1-4). The rich came to be seen and with great fanfare *threw* in their bags of money. A poor widow came and quietly put in her two small coins. Jesus told His disciples, "She gave more." She gave all she had to live on while the others made a show of giving out of their abundance.

Frances Ridley Havergal wrote one of her most well-known hymns, "Take My Life and Let It Be," in 1874. It was not until 1878, the year before she died, that the lines were put into print. When she read the second stanza—"Take my silver and my gold, not a mite would I withhold"—she was suddenly convicted of her failure to do just that. She had an amazing collection of exquisite jewelry, most of which came by gift or inheritance. Immediately she packed the jewels and sent them to her church's missionary society. Then, just to be sure, she included a check to cover the monetary value of the jewels she had chosen to keep! "I don't think I need to tell you that I have never packed a box with such pleasure!" she exclaimed.[3]

# MAKE, SAVE, GIVE

Several years ago the then prime minister of Great Britain Margaret Thatcher addressed the General Assembly of the

Church of Scotland. She talked about the creation of wealth and quoted John Wesley as saying, "Make all you can and save all you can." She didn't complete Wesley's thought, however, because he went on to say, "And give all you can."

There is a story of a retired farmer who, upon hearing Wesley preach on this, later remarked, "I liked his first point, I loved his second point, and then with his third he went and spoilt it all."[4]

John Wesley lived on £28 (i.e., $45) a year when he was a student at Oxford University in the 1720s. When his income rose to £30 a year, he gave £2 away. When it rose to £60 a year, he lived on £28 and gave £32 away. When it rose to £90, he gave away £62. From the sale of books alone, John Wesley gave away between £30,000 and £40,000. He told Samuel Bradburn, one of his preachers, that he never gave away less than £1,000 a year.[5]

Like the apostle Paul, Wesley learned to be content—whatever the circumstances. Money had no hold on his soul. Such freedom may sound like foolishness to us; but when Wesley heard that his home had been destroyed by fire, he exclaimed, "The Lord's house burned; one less responsibility for me."

When his friend Samuel Bradburn was once in difficult financial circumstances, John Wesley sent him the following letter:

Dear Sammy,
    Trust in the Lord and do good, so shalt thou dwell in the land and verily thou shalt be fed.
Yours affectionately,
John Wesley

Wesley enclosed two £5 notes. The reply was prompt:

Rev. and Dear Sir,
    I have often been struck with the beauty of the passage

of scripture quoted in your good letter, but I must confess that I never saw such useful expository notes on it
before.

I am, reverend and dear sir, your obedient and grateful
servant,

S. Bradburn

Shortly before Wesley died he wrote these moving words:
"For upwards of 86 years I have kept my accounts exactly. I will
not attempt it any longer, being satisfied with the continual conviction that I did save all I can, and that I did give all I can, that
is all I have." The earthly possessions he left when he died
amounted to £6 in money, six silver spoons and 129,000
Methodists.[6]

It is often well said that it is impossible to outgive God. He
is no man's debtor. "Test me in this" is His challenge (Mal. 3:10).
As one farmer known for his generous giving put it, "I just take
my shovel and shovel into God's barn, and He takes His shovel
and shovels into my barn. I have discovered that God has a big-
ger shovel."

May God deliver us from the mean-spirited, tightfisted attitude that strives to keep our pockets full, yet leaves our hearts
empty. For a tight fist is often the sign of an empty heart.

I like the story of the millionaire who complained to his
minister that in the past year he had earned $500,000, which
meant that he should tithe $50,000. He said it was far too much
and could not afford it. The minister smiled and replied, "I
understand. Let's take it to God and pray about it." So he prayed,
"Dear Lord, you see my brother's predicament, so please reduce
his income until he can afford to give properly to you."

John Bunyan, writer of the Christian classic *The Pilgrim's
Progress*, put it like this: "A man was there, tho' some did count

him mad, the more he cast away the more he had." Solomon says it even better:

> One man gives freely, yet gains even more; another withholds unduly, but comes to poverty (Prov. 11:24).

My wife and I learned this lesson powerfully during our time in Bible college. We received a very small grant to live on—half of what was usual because of government cutbacks. We were thankful for what we received, though, because many of our friends did not receive any grant money at all. For a while we managed quite well as God met our needs, but then things started to go wrong. Bills began piling up, and we were only halfway through our course.

When my wife and I discussed and prayed about the matter, we discovered something disturbing: In the midst of our busy lives, each of us thought that the other was seeing to our weekly giving. For many weeks, maybe months, we had neglected to honor God in our finances.

Let me be clear on this: God was not bringing judgment on us for our honest mistake. But He had allowed pressures to build in order to get our attention and help us put things right. We decided we would make good on all we should have given—but this was easier said than done. Our solution was to give 20 percent of our income for a while. After a few months, everything turned around. We did not become wealthy, but we had a car bought for us, our bills paid and every need met.

## GIVING UNLOCKS BLESSING FOR THE CHURCH

Some of the world's largest churches are in Seoul, South Korea. There you will find the biggest Presbyterian, Methodist and

Pentecostal churches. The largest of the churches is the Yoido Full Gospel Church, which has known phenomenal growth and in 1998 had 750,000 members. Dr. David Yonggi Cho, the senior minister, stresses the vital importance of prayer in his best-selling book *Prayer: Key to Revival*. He also tells the amazing story of how the church building was constructed in 1973, and how God released the people in overwhelming generosity and sacrifice to enable its completion:

> At that time the dollar was devalued which caused the Korean *won* to suffer and the nation entered into a deep recession. Then the oil crisis hit, worsening the already fragile economy. Our people lost their jobs and our income went down.
>
> Having signed contracts with the construction company, and experiencing an unprecedented increase in building costs, I suffered greatly, seeing the possibility of a financial collapse. Despondently, I sat in my unfinished church building, wishing the still bare rafters would just fall on me. During this crucial time in my ministry, a group from our church went to the property and started building a place to pray, mainly for their suffering pastor. Although I saw the need for this in our church, my concern was the added expenses that kept piling up on my desk. Seeing that only a miraculous intervention of God would deliver us from a catastrophe, I joined the intercessors at Prayer Mountain.
>
> One evening, while we were meeting to pray on the ground floor of our unfinished church, several hundred joined me in prayer. An old woman walked slowly in my direction. As she approached the platform, I noticed that tears were filling her eyes. She bowed and said,

"Pastor, I want to give these items to you so that you may sell them for a few pennies to help with our building fund." I looked down, and in her hands were an old rice bowl and a pair of chopsticks.

Then I said to her, "Sister, I can't take these necessities from you!"

"But Pastor, I am an old woman. I have nothing of value to give to my Lord; yet, Jesus has graciously saved me. These items are the only things in the world I possess!" she exclaimed, tears now freely flowing down her wrinkled cheeks. "You must let me give these to Jesus. I can place my rice on old newspapers and I can use my hands to feed myself. I know that I will die soon, so I don't want to meet Jesus without giving Him something on this earth." As she finished speaking, everyone there began to weep openly. The Holy Spirit's presence filled the place and we all began to pray in the Spirit.

A businessman at the back of the group was deeply moved and said, "Pastor Cho, I want to buy that rice bowl and chopsticks for one thousand dollars!"

With that, everyone started to pledge their possessions. My wife and I sold our small home and gave the money to the church. This spirit of giving saved us from financial ruin.[7]

It has been estimated that only 20 percent of the Church worldwide tithes, and the average tithe of church members is 2.5 percent.[8] If all God's people gave as they should, not only would there be a financial explosion for missions but also tremendous blessing poured out upon the Church. A great breakthrough and release of giftings and ministries would come as people experienced liberation in their giving. A more powerful sense of

God's presence would come as He would be honored in our giving. Worshiping God is not only about singing; it is about a lifestyle of giving (see Rom. 12:1). Worship means not only taking out our songbooks; it also means getting out our checkbooks.

JOHN D. ROCKEFELLER WAS ONCE ASKED, "HOW MUCH MONEY DOES IT TAKE TO MAKE SOMEONE HAPPY?" HIS ANSWER: "ALWAYS A LITTLE BIT MORE."

## MORE BLESSED TO GIVE THAN TO RECEIVE

John Davison Rockefeller was one of the richest men the world has ever known. He was once asked, "How much money does it take to make someone happy?"

His reply is very revealing. He answered, "Always a little bit more."

By 33 he had made his first million dollars. Making money was his obsession. At 43 he controlled the greatest business empire in the world, and by 53 he had become the world's first billionaire.

Such achievements did not come without a cost, for in the process he had bartered his own happiness and health. He developed alopecia, a condition in which not only the hair of the head drops out but also most of the hair from the eyelashes and eyebrows. One of his biographers said that he looked like an Egyptian mummy. His weekly income was a million dollars, but his digestion was so bad that he could eat only crackers and milk. He was hated in the business world, known for crushing those who stood in his way. He was so despised in the oil fields of Pennsylvania that the men whom he had pauperized hanged him in effigy. He had to be surrounded by bodyguards day and night.

His biographers tell the story about one of the army of groundskeepers at his mansion, Pocantino. The gentleman was given a five-dollar bill as a Christmas bonus, only to have it docked for spending the holiday with his wife and children instead of being at work. Friends who were invited to stay for the weekend at his 700-acre estate at Forest Hill were astonished to receive a bill when they returned home.

His massive wealth brought him neither peace nor happiness. As he sought to protect and control his riches, he discovered that they were destroying him. He could not sleep; he enjoyed nothing. When he was 53, biographer Ida Tarbell wrote of him, "An awful age was in his face. He was the oldest man I have ever seen."[9] The crackers and milk that he glumly swallowed could no longer hold together his skinny body and restless soul. It was generally agreed that he would not live another year, and newspaper writers had his obituary already written and in their files.

It was during those long sleepless nights that he realized he would not be able to take even one of his thin dimes with him into the next world. For the first time in his life he recognized that money was not a commodity to be hoarded but something to be shared for the benefit of others. Like Scrooge in Charles Dickens's *A Christmas Carol,* he lost no time in using his money to start blessing others. He began to look for worthy causes he could help. He established the Rockefeller Foundation so that some of his fortune could be channeled into needed areas.

He helped rid the American South of its greatest economic and physical scourge, hookworm. We can thank him every time a life is helped by an injection of penicillin, because it was his contributions that aided the development of the drug. His wealth sparked research that has saved multitudes from malaria, tuberculosis, diphtheria and many other diseases. He gave a large donation to rebuild the University of Chicago and insisted that the new university should be "aggressively Christian with no infidel teachers."

Something remarkable began to happen to him when his attitude changed from one of getting to giving. The bitterness and selfishness went out of his life and a miracle began to occur. He started to sleep at night, to eat normally and to enjoy life again. Not only did he make it to his 54th birthday, but he lived until he was 98 years old![10]

The world-famous psychiatrist Dr. Karl Menninger referred to giving money as a good criterion of a person's mental health. He said that generous people are rarely mentally ill. He once asked a wealthy patient, "What on earth are you going to do with all that money?"

The patient replied, "Just worry about it, I suppose."

Dr. Menninger went on, "Well, do you get that much pleasure out of worrying about it?"

"No," responded the patient, "but I get such terror when I think of giving some of it to somebody."

Dr. Alfred Adler, another famous psychiatrist, said, "I suppose all the ills of human personality can be traced back to one thing, namely not understanding the meaning of the statement, 'It is more blessed to give than to receive.'"

# THE ABILITY TO PRODUCE WEALTH

But remember the LORD your God, for it is he who gives you the ability to produce wealth, and so confirms his covenant, which he swore to your forefathers, as it is today (Deut. 8:18).

With how much can God trust you? If He gave you the ability to create wealth like John D. Rockefeller, would you become greedy or generous? Selfish or selfless? God is looking for people through whom He is able to channel wealth for the work of His kingdom here on earth. Are you such a person?

Only recently I was speaking with a wealthy Canadian businessman who owns 27 companies. He told me that many years ago God called him to minister to the poor around the world. This businessman gives a great deal of his time to this, as well as 50 percent of his personal income and his companies' profits. The more he has given, the more God has blessed his businesses.

Let me ask you a few more questions:

Do you ever feel threatened by the subject of money?

Are you afraid you have too little or fearful you may have too much?

Do future needs and uncertainties frighten you?

Are you fearful others might overestimate your wealth and arrive at the conclusion that you are greedy?

We need to take these issues seriously if we want God to make us producers of wealth.

Our inability to relate properly to money can often come from childhood memories. Many reading this have grown up in a family where there was severe financial hardship. You may remember arguments about money, your mother's tears of desperation and your father's anger and frustration. Because of this you have determined that *your* family will not suffer. We all must ask ourselves, *Am I in danger of developing a hoarding, holding spirit? Is it part of my nature? Am I ever able to enjoy and be content with what I have?*

Others have grown up in affluence and may now feel guilty about having had too much. You may be very aware of the dangers wealth can bring and find yourself unable to enjoy what you possess.

Only when we come to terms with what has shaped our attitudes toward money are we able to act upon the biblical call to financial stewardship.

When God brought His people out of slavery in Egypt, it was not so they could limp along, barely surviving. The Promised Land was one of abundant provision. God's loving purpose was to give His people a land flowing with milk and honey—with grapes so large it took two men to carry one cluster (see Num. 13:23).

In the book of Deuteronomy, Moses reminds the children of Israel of how God provided for them and protected them in the past. He looks to the future and warns them to keep God's laws and to follow His ways as they enter a land not only full of blessing but also filled with the evil and occult practices of the peoples living there. In Deuteronomy 8, Moses warns them about some of the temptations they will experience, saying, "If you ever forget the LORD your God and follow other gods and worship and bow down to them, I testify against you today that you will surely be destroyed" (Deut. 8:19). It is God who gave His people what they did not work for and the ability and skill to create even more wealth.

Throughout history the Jews not only have demonstrated the will to survive, but they also have had the skill to succeed. They have provided the world with some of its greatest thinkers, inventors, scientists, industrialists, artists, filmmakers, researchers, pioneers and benefactors. They have had the ability to create and accumulate wealth out of all proportion to their numbers and circumstances. Without the Jews, advances in the banking world would have been delayed for centuries. And without banking, great government enterprises and the wholesale expansion of industry would have been impossible. It was the Jewish House of Rothschild that made the stock market an international institution.

If God gives the ability to produce wealth, what then do we make of all the warnings in Scripture about the dangers of riches? The Lord says, "Don't weary yourself trying to get rich. Why waste your time? For riches can disappear as though they had the wings of a bird" (Prov. 23:4,5, *TLB*).

The ability to produce wealth is different from the pursuit of riches. Anyone who has a passion to be rich for riches' sake is in grave danger, but a person who is able to produce wealth for the purposes of God is a great blessing.

God's people should seek to excel in their work and businesses so that God is glorified. If they do, the reward of their labor is not only a blessing to their lives but also to God's kingdom. Ask God to help you in your job. Work hard and determine that whatever you do, you will do it to the best of your ability. Whatever your hand finds to do, do it with all your strength and remember that no farmer plowed a field by turning it over in his mind.

Let your boss see God's favor on you, even if he or she does not understand it. God eventually blessed Joseph in Egypt in whatever he did (see Gen. 41:41-49); the same was true for Daniel in Babylon (see Dan. 6:28). Through their ability to produce wealth and administer wisely, even in foreign lands, God's purposes were established.

If you own a business, give it to God and ask for His ability to make that business a testimony to His glory. When people ask you how you have done so well, tell them what God has done. Ask God for wisdom in your business transactions—He will give it to you. God will even give you warnings about what to move into and what to avoid. Pray about the staff you hire. Ask God to send you people with skill and ability like the people He sent to Moses to build the Tabernacle (see Exod. 35,36). Determine in your heart that, with God's help, your business will be a channel of provision for the gospel.

Many people dream of making a million dollars by the time they are 30, 40 or 50. Why not pray that you will have been able to *give* a million dollars by then instead?

*Notes*
1. Leonard Ravenhill, *Why Revival Tarries* (London: Send the Light Trust, 1972), p. 8.
2. Hannah Ward and Jennifer Wild, *The Lion Christian Quotation Collection* (London: Lion Publishing PLC, 1997), p. 242.
3. Walter B. Knight, comp., *Knight's Master Book of New Illustrations* (Grand Rapids, MI: Eerdmans Publishing Co., 1956), p. 249.
4. Graham Twelttree, *Drive the Point Home* (England: Monarch Publishing, 1994), p. 136.
5. A. Naismith, *1200 More Notes, Quotes and Anecdotes* (London: Pickering and Inglis Ltd., 1975), p. 29.
6. Tom Rees, *Money Talks* (London: Billing and Sons Ltd., 1963), p. 30.
7. David Yonggi Cho, *Prayer: Key to Revival* (Waco, TX: Word Publishing, 1987).
8. Joseph Miller, "The Resources of the Church," *Church Planter* (October/December 1994).
9. Robert C. Savage, *Pocket Wisdom* (Minneapolis, MN: Worldwide Publications, 1984), p. 85.
10. Margaret Nicholas, *The World's Wealthiest Losers* (London: Chancellor Press, 1997).

# CHAPTER 2

# GIVING IN THE OLD TESTAMENT

*The limit of giving is to be the limit of our ability to give.*

C. S. LEWIS

Does the Bible clearly state that we must give to the Lord? If so, how much? The Old Testament guides us to give 10 percent of our gross income, but what does the New Testament say?

Before we address these questions, let us start with a definition of what we mean by tithing. For our purposes, a general definition is *prayerful, obedient, grace-filled giving.*

The first mention of giving in the Bible occurs more than 400 years before the Law was given through Moses, taking place after Abraham had rescued his nephew Lot and recovered all the people and possessions that had been plundered from Sodom and Gomorrah by their enemies. Melchizedek, king of Jerusalem, met Abraham after his victory and received from him a 10th of the spoils he had won (see Heb. 7:4).

Abraham later refused the reward offered to him by the king of Sodom.

> Then Melchizedek king of Salem brought out bread and wine. He was priest of God Most High, and he blessed Abram, saying, "Blessed be Abram by God Most High, Creator of heaven and earth. And blessed be God Most High, who delivered your enemies into your hand." Then Abram gave him a tenth of everything.
>
> The king of Sodom said to Abram, "Give me the people and keep the goods for yourself."
>
> But Abram said to the king of Sodom, "I have raised my hand to the LORD, God Most High, Creator of heaven and earth, and have taken an oath that I will accept nothing belonging to you, not even a thread or the thong of a sandal, so that you will never be able to say, 'I made Abram rich'" (Gen. 14:18-23).

Not long after this, Abraham may have been contemplating his difficult and dangerous circumstances. He had not only made new friends but also new enemies of those he had defeated. He was also discouraged because he had no son who would be his heir. The word of the Lord came to him in a vision: "Do not be afraid, Abram. I am your shield, your very great reward" (Gen. 15:1). God Himself would protect Abraham and give him the son he longed for.

It was with this son, Isaac, that Abraham's greatest test would come. At God's command he took Isaac, now a young man, to make a sacrifice on Mount Moriah (see Gen. 22:1-19). After journeying three days they came to the mountain. Leaving the donkey with two of his servants, Abraham and Isaac ascended the mountain alone. Abraham took the wood for the burnt offering and placed it on his son, while he carried the fire and the knife. Abraham built an altar and placed the wood upon it. Isaac, trusting his father, allowed himself to be bound and placed upon the altar. This clearly foreshadowed the time when God would give His Son on a hill just a short distance from this very spot.

Isaac watched as his father took out his knife to offer him as the greatest sacrifice of his love. But God stopped Abraham—this was only a test. God did not want Isaac on Mount Carmel; He wanted Abraham, whose willingness showed complete surrender of everything he had.

# A GOLDEN CALF OR A TABERNACLE?

When Moses led the Israelites out of Egypt, God saw to it that 400 years of hard labor did not go without payment. As the Hebrews left the fertile Nile River valley, they were loaded down with the treasures of Egypt. What good was gold in the desert? It was to be for both a test and a testimony.

There are two significant accounts of what the Israelites did with their wealth that teach us a great deal. When Moses was on Mount Sinai with God, the people rebelled. They took their treasure and threw it into a furnace to make a calf of gold, an act of idolatry that brought with it the judgment of God (see Exod. 32).

At the same time God was giving instructions to Moses about building the Tabernacle, the devil was inciting the people to use their wealth to make an idol. Satan uses the love of money not only to trap people in its pursuit, but also to hinder the purposes of God's kingdom by restricting use of money for His purposes. The devil fears what the release of finances will do for God's work and the blessing it will bring into people's lives.

By the time of Exodus 35, the people had returned to the ways of the Lord. So when Moses called for the people to give to the building of the Tabernacle, they brought so much that he had to tell them to stop. (What a problem to have!) They came with gold, silver, bronze, fine cloth, animal skins, fragrances and incense to make a dwelling where God would come in His glory (see Exod. 35:5—36:7).

# THE OLD TESTAMENT AND TITHING

There were three tithes required in the Old Testament. There was the festival tithe, which was provision for the people to attend and enjoy the major feasts (see Deut. 12:5-19; 14:22-27). There was a benevolence tithe, given every three years to help the poor (see Deut. 14:28,29). The major tithe was the Levitical tithe (see Lev. 27:30-32; Num. 18:20-32). This was established under the Law but did not originate from it.

Under Mosaic Law, the tithe consisted of the "increase" (Deut. 14:22, *NKJV*) of the produce of the land, from the harvest at the end of the year (see Lev. 27:30-32). What the word "increase" (i.e., profit or gain) means precisely is disputed. Though often debated, common acceptance among scholars is that for Christians today, the tithe refers to 10 percent of one's gross income.

Jewish rabbinical tradition says that a tithing cycle of seven years—the *Shemmitah* cycle—corresponded with a seven-year crop cultivation cycle. Each seventh year was to be a "Sabbath Year of Rest" for the land (see Lev. 25:1-7). This Shemmitah seven-year cycle included three kinds of tithes. The "first tithe" (or *ma'asher roshi* in Hebrew) was for the maintenance of the Levites (see Num. 18:20-32). The priestly Levites had no "inheritance," or land to farm, hence no means of support. In exchange for their service as teachers of the Law and in tabernacle service, the tithe was instituted.

The common rabbinical interpretation called the second year's tithe the "second tithe" (ma'aser sheni) and said that this tithe was for the annual purpose of sending the farmer, his family, his servants and the Levites on pilgrimage to the central sanctuary to rejoice in the blessing of the Lord (see Deut. 12:1-28; 26:1-11).

The Bible mentions a "year of the tithe" in the third year (Deut. 26:12). This is what the rabbis called the tithe for the poor (ma'aser ani) and was collected at the end of every three years at storehouses in the many local villages. This tithe was for sustenance of the Levite, the fatherless, the widow and the stranger (see Deut. 14:28,29; 26:12-15).

The Levites were to then tithe from what was tithed to them ("a tithe of the tithe") to the high priest at the central sanctuary (see Num. 18:26). This tithe of the tithe, which amounted to one percent of the farmers' tithes, was just a small part of the total inventory of gifts and offerings that were brought to the central sanctuary. The prophet Malachi criticized the Levitical "priests" for neglecting to tithe what had been tithed to them (see Mal. 1:6; 2:1; 3:3).

After the Torah (the first five books of the Bible), tithing is rarely mentioned in the Bible. In the pre-exilic writings, tithing without proper reverence for God is condemned (see Amos 4:4). Tithing seems to have fallen into disuse, but it was reinstituted during the revival during Hezekiah's reign (see 2 Chron. 31:5).

Tithing ("firstfruits") is mentioned in the wisdom literature in the promise of Proverbs 3:9,10: "Honor the LORD with your wealth, with the firstfruits of all your crops; then your barns will be filled to overflowing, and your vats will brim over with new wine," echoing the language of blessings for obedience and curses for disobedience found in Leviticus 26 and Deuteronomy 28 and 30.

Among the post-exilic books of the Bible, tithing is mentioned six times in the book of Nehemiah, describing part of the effort to rebuild the Temple after the Babylonian captivity (see Neh. 10:37,38; 13:12). Tithing is also mentioned twice in the book of Malachi the prophet, who sees the withholding of tithes—a charge focused on the Levites but including all the people—as "robbing" God (Mal. 3:8).

Yet another aspect of tithing had to do with the harvesting of fields. It was forbidden for farmers to harvest the corners of their fields, so the poor and travelers along the roads could have something to eat (see Lev. 19:9,10; Deut. 24:21). This "law of gleaning" was an obligatory form of charity that was required of landowners but not of wage earners.

The primary purposes for tithing in the Old Testament were to worship God, showing one's love for Him; to show love for one's neighbor through justice, mercy and faithfulness, as Jesus later points out (see Matt. 23:23); to provide food for the landless Levites, who led the people in worship and taught the Law; for fellowship and pilgrimage to the central sanctuary for all people in towns and villages; and to set up the villages as outposts of mercy and food for the poor and travelers in a harsh environment. What a beautiful demonstration of God's faithfulness through His people!

In his book *Tithing: A Call to Serious Biblical Giving*, Dr. R. T. Kendall, pastor of Westminster Chapel in London, calculated that the average amount given to God in tithes and offerings each year in the Old Testament might have been as much as a quarter of one's annual income. In describing the three tithes, Kendall asserts that these Jews gave at least 23.5 percent of their income![1]

God taught His people that they were to honor Him with the tithe and to bring sacrifices and offerings. This was how the priesthood was supported, but more importantly it was the way the Israelites honored God and placed Him first in their lives. Yet sadly and significantly, it is possible to measure Israel's spiritual decline with the people's attitude toward their giving. The prophets—two of them being Haggai and Malachi—had a great deal to say about this.

# HAGGAI ON GIVING

From around 605 B.C. Judah was under the rule of Babylon. Spiritual decline had led to the destruction of Solomon's magnificent Temple and the burning of Jerusalem. Seventy years of captivity in Babylon passed, but Jeremiah had prophesied that there would come a return of the people to their land (see Jer. 25:11,12; 29:10). Daniel read about this prophecy and with just two years to go until the prophecy's anticipated completion, he prayed and sought God regarding its fulfillment (see Dan. 9:2,3). Then a miracle happened. Under an edict of King Cyrus of Persia, who had defeated and captured Babylon, a group of Israelites numbering 40,000 to 50,000 were allowed to return to their homeland (see Ezra 1:1-4).

Led by Zerubbabel the governor and Jeshua the high priest, they began the restoration of Jerusalem by building the foundation of the Temple (see Ezra 3:8-10). This was laid almost straightaway, but the work was then delayed for more than 15 years. It is during this period that the prophets Haggai and Zechariah brought God's word to the nation. Only the Temple's foundation had been laid as the people had concentrated on building their own homes and securing their own financial welfare. It is interesting to note that while there was hostile opposition from neighboring kingdoms to the rebuilding of God's Temple, there seemed to be little opposition to the people building their luxurious homes. Obviously the devil was not quite so bothered by this.

Haggai thundered forth and urged the people to complete the task of rebuilding the Temple. He pulled no punches as he told them why they had holes in their pockets and had become impoverished:

> Is it a time for you yourselves to be living in your paneled houses, while this house remains a ruin? Now this is what the LORD Almighty says: "Give careful thought to your ways. You have planted much, but have harvested little. You eat, but never have enough. You drink, but never have your fill. You put on clothes, but are not warm. You earn wages, only to put them in a purse with holes in it" (Hag. 1:4-6).

Strong stuff! But that was just the start. Haggai went on:

> "Give careful thought to your ways. Go up into the mountains and bring down timber and build the house, so that I may take pleasure in it and be honored," says the LORD. "You expected much, but see, it turned out to be little. What you brought home, I blew away. Why?" declares the LORD Almighty. "Because of my house, which remains a ruin, while each of you is busy with his own house. Therefore, because of you the heavens have withheld their dew and the earth its crops. I called for a drought on the fields and the mountains, on the grain, the new wine, the oil and whatever the ground produces,

on men and cattle, and on the labor of your hands" (Hag. 1:7-11).

They had started in the Spirit and were finishing in the flesh. God's desire was to establish them in the land. He had brought them back and desired to abundantly bless them, but they had become caught up with themselves and materialism. God's Temple had been neglected. They now had to go up into the hills to get wood because there was none left on the plains—it had been used for their paneled homes.

There is nothing wrong with living in a beautiful home; it can be the grace of God's blessing. But it is tragic if our home ends up owning us and we become so caught up with ourselves that we lose track of our priorities and give God second place.

The work on the Temple was resumed and completed with the wonderful promise that the glory of the new house would be "greater than the glory of the former house." God Almighty declared, "In this place I will grant peace" (Hag. 2:9).

**THERE IS NOTHING WRONG WITH LIVING IN A BEAUTIFUL HOME. BUT IT IS TRAGIC IF OUR HOME ENDS UP OWNING US.**

# MALACHI ON GIVING

The people in Malachi's day had again become spiritually cold and complacent. Almost a hundred years had passed since the Temple and city walls of Jerusalem had been rebuilt, and spiritual lethargy had taken hold of the people. They were sacrificing animals that were crippled and diseased. What was no use to them they presented to God. They brought not their best but their worst. It was clearly stated in the Law that they were to give God the best of their best (see Exod. 23:19). Instead they brought the worst of the worst, revealing a great deal about the condition of their hearts.

Listen to God's heart as He declared to the priests, who were supposed to be the spiritual leaders of the people, that He did not want their rejects or second best:

> "A son honors his father, and a servant his master. If I am a father, where is the honor due me? If I am a master, where is the respect due me?" says the LORD Almighty. "It is you, O priests, who show contempt for my name. But you ask, 'How have we shown contempt for your name?' You place defiled food on my altar. But you ask, 'How have we defiled you?' By saying that the LORD'S table is contemptible. When you bring blind animals for sacrifice, is that not wrong? When you sacrifice crippled or diseased animals, is that not wrong? Try offering them to your governor! Would he be pleased with you? Would he accept you?" says the LORD Almighty (Mal. 1:6-8).

Some of the priests gave to God as if tipping a waiter. God's response to this type of attitude is spoken clearly in Malachi 1:10: "Oh, that one of you would shut the temple doors, so that you would not light useless fires on my altar! I am not pleased with you." But the sin of the people in giving their rejects and second best was not all. The people also withheld their tithes.

God told them that if they would turn back and if they would honor Him, they would live under an open heaven of His blessing (see Mal. 3:10). He promised to provide for them and protect them; the devourer would be rebuked and they would be honored and respected wherever they went: "Then all the nations will call you blessed, for yours will be a delightful land" (Mal. 3:12).

Note where the people were told to bring their tithes and offerings: to God's storehouse. We need to seriously pray and decide where our storehouse is as we are continually being challenged to give to many worthy Christian and charitable causes. The primary place of our giving should be to our local church, the storehouse from which we are spiritually fed. This does not mean that we should give to nothing else. On the contrary, let us look for good ground to sow seed into with other missions and ministries. Personally, however, I believe that the money we give to other ministries should be our offerings and not our tithes.

How tragic—yet revealing—that the Old Testament begins with God giving man almost everything and ends with man unwilling to give God hardly anything. It starts with God giving His best and ends with man giving his worst. It begins with God bestowing His blessing and ends with God once again desiring to bless. But tragically, the last word of the Old Testament is the word "curse" (Mal. 4:6).

Note
1. R. T. Kendall, *Tithing: A Call to Serious Biblical Giving* (London: Hodder and Stoughton, 1982).

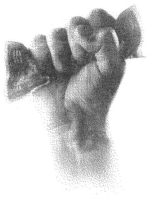

# CHAPTER 3

# GIVING IN THE NEW TESTAMENT

*What I gave I have, what I spent I had, what I kept I lost.*

MARTIN LUTHER

In the first century A.D. the world was pouring its riches into the lap of Rome. Merchandise was brought in from every land and across every sea. Rome's opulence and extravagance knew no bounds as the empire raped and pillaged the world to feed its insatiable appetite for more and more pleasure and luxury.

The money possessed and the money spent was colossal. One of Emperor Nero's freedmen could regard a man with a fortune of the equivalent of $1 million as a pauper. One citizen, Apicius, squandered a fortune of millions on refined debauchery and committed suicide when he had only $250,000 left, because he could not live on such a pittance. Nero declared that the only use of money was to squander it and, in just a few years, he managed to squander the equivalent of more than $50 million.

At one banquet he gave, his Egyptian roses alone cost $75,000.[1]

Nero reveled in earthly possessions and set his heart upon them. From his splendid throne as ruler of the Roman Empire, he commanded that gorgeous porches a mile long be built around the palace. The ceiling of his banquet hall was equipped at great expense with hidden showers that lightly sprayed perfume upon all who came to visit him. Even his mules were shod with silver.

Whenever he traveled, a thousand chariots accompanied him, and he refused to wear the same garment twice no matter its cost or beauty. Taxing the people unmercifully, he was able to pay extravagant sums of money to anyone who could devise new methods for entertaining him. Yet with all his riches and splendor he was a miserable, gloomy, spiteful and dissatisfied man. The immense wealth he had amassed could not satisfy his soul. Nero committed suicide by ordering an attendant to stab him before the Senate's order of his execution could be carried out.

The Roman historian Suetonius described and denounced the lifestyle of Rome's emperors. Of Emperor Caligula he wrote, "In reckless extravagance he outdid the prodigals of all times in ingenuity, inventing a new sort of baths and unnatural varieties of food and feasts. He would bathe in hot or cold perfumed oils, drink pearls of great price dissolved in vinegar, and set before his guests loaves and meats of gold."[2]

Rome was a city of extraordinary gluttony. Dishes of peacocks' brains and nightingales' tongues were set before the guests at banquets. Vitellius, who was emperor for less than a year, succeeded in spending an estimated $15 million, mainly on food.

Despite such wealth and opulence, most lives were empty and miserable. They sought continually to invent new games and ways of pleasure with sexual depravity of almost every kind.

They pampered their bodies and in the process pauperized their souls.

The pursuit and possession of wealth was not only a Roman passion. Money's power and false promises have affected every nation through the millennia. This is why Jesus and the New Testament writers referred to money so often. Jesus only spoke more often about the kingdom of God. He taught that money can free you or imprison you, be a blessing or a curse. Jesus' warnings are many:

Woe to you who are rich (Luke 6:24).

Ye cannot serve God and mammon (Luke 16:13, *KJV*).

Do not lay up for yourselves treasures on earth (Matt. 6:19, *NKJV*).

It is easier for a camel to go through the eye of a needle than for a rich man to enter the kingdom of God (Matt. 19:24).

Take heed and beware of covetousness (Luke 12:15, *NKJV*).

Sell your possessions and give to the poor (Luke 12:33).

Give to everyone who asks of you. And from him who takes away your goods do not ask them back (Luke 6:30, *NKJV*).

A danger with such Scriptures is for us to either use them to induce guilt or treat them too lightly. Some critics insert contextual qualifications to explain why such passages are not relevant for our day, or they find some other reason to interpret and explain them away. We must not do this.

First, we must allow the Word of God to speak to us and listen to what it says. We are to interpret and apply the words in the light of their context and culture—and then heed the warnings. In each case, we must allow the voice of the Holy Spirit to minister to our hearts.

Jesus also taught that we can use our money to glorify God and bless others. When Zacchaeus was freed from having a greedy spirit, Jesus joyfully announced, "Today salvation has come to this house" (Luke 19:9). When Jesus was anointed with expensive perfumes, He rebuked those who criticized the notorious woman and praised her for showing such extravagant love (see Matt. 26:6-12). The Bible speaks volumes on the subject of money:

- One in four verses in the Gospels of Matthew, Mark and Luke refer to wealth. They contain 2,899 verses, of which 724 verses have a reference to money—more verses than in the whole Gospel of Mark.
- There are 7,931 verses in the New Testament, 1,332 of which refer to money—one verse in every six. That is more verses than the books of Galatians; Ephesians; Philippians; Colossians; 1 and 2 Thessalonians; 1 and 2 Timothy; Titus; Philemon; James; 1 and 2 Peter; 1, 2 and 3 John and Jude *combined*!
- Sixteen of the 38 parables that Jesus told contain a reference to wealth and money.
- Money is mentioned in the Bible 2,085 times, more than heaven, hell, love and faith combined. There are 500 verses on prayer and 500 verses on faith.
- The first recorded sin in the Early Church had to do

with two people lying regarding money (see Acts 5:1-11). The first recorded sin after Joshua led the people into the Promised Land was when Achan hid gold under the floor of his tent (see Josh. 7).

One of the saddest people in the entire Bible is Elisha's servant Gehazi. As told in 2 Kings 5, the Lord used Elisha to heal Namaan of leprosy, but Elisha declined any reward. Afterward though, Gehazi ran after Namaan to claim the financial reward and then keep it for himself. When Gehazi returned to Elisha, Gehazi lied about where he had been, so God judged him by striking him with leprosy.

What is worse, the prophetic anointing that came from Elijah to Elisha could well have been passed to Gehazi. As Elisha received the double portion, which was the place of the firstborn or leader of the prophets, so too Gehazi was in line. Gehazi literally exchanged the anointing for a bag of gold, but he as given leprosy instead.

First Timothy 6:10 is probably the most misquoted verse in the whole Bible: "For the love of money is a root of all kinds of evil." Notice that it does not say money is evil, but the *love* of money. Not all bad things have to do with the love of money, but a great deal of evil does. When we give to the Lord joyfully, the process helps to break the tyranny and power that money can have over us.

# NEW TESTAMENT GIVING

"We want to give you a gift." Those words bring a smile to everyone's face—but this was special.

Jan and I had been invited to supper after the Sunday evening service. We had recently left Bible college and been appointed to a church to assist the senior pastor. The family we were with that night had started attending our church only a few months before we arrived and had been very helpful and friendly to us.

"This is for you to help buy another car," they said. "God has told us to bless you." The husband handed me a check for £1,000. We desperately needed to get another car, as the engine in ours had died and I longed to bury it. We felt overwhelmed, not just at the money but also at the love of this couple who hardly knew us. Most of all, we were humbled by the fact that our heavenly Father knows everything we have need of and had provided in such a special way.

On the way home I reflected upon the fact that this was the second time God had blessed us with a car as a gift. I said to Jan, "God's blessing upon us must have something to do with the principle of sowing and reaping." Before we went to college, we used our cars to transport children and the elderly back and forth to church. I had also loaned my car to our pastor for four months when his was in need of repair. Then, along with some others from the church, we helped the pastor buy a new car. We were learning that we may not reap *when* or *where* we sow, but God will always see to it that we will reap *what* we sow.

# GIVING IS SEED WE SOW

As we have already seen with Abraham and Melchizedek (see Gen. 14:18-20), the principle of tithing was established before the Law, although its practice became incorporated into the Law. Jesus affirmed and endorsed the practice of selfless giving when He condemned the Pharisees who, though conscientious in their tithing, were ignoring other matters of the Law (see

Matt. 23:23-28). Jesus did not have to do a lot of teaching on tithing because it was woven so deeply into Jewish thinking and belief. He only had to affirm the practice of such giving.

Paul also encouraged the Corinthian Christians to give in a systematic and proportionate way: "On the first day of every week, each one of you should set aside a sum of money in keeping with his income" (1 Cor. 16:2).

The Early Church fathers—Origen, Jerome, Chrysostom and others—taught and practiced tithing. The Council of Trent in 1545 not only encouraged tithing but also threatened to excommunicate those who withheld tithes.[3]

Nowhere does the New Testament give a specific percentage for how much we should give. But imagine for a moment a Jewish family in A.D. 50 that has recently embraced salvation through Christ. They sit down at the beginning of the week to work out their finances. All their lives they have been bound by the Mosaic Law, paying their tithes, Temple dues and taxes, bringing sacrifices and offerings. But even though all these things continue at the Temple, they now have in Christ the ultimate sacrifice *once for all*. The entire ritual and sacrificial system are now seen as a mere shadow of the fulfillment that has come.[4]

Having found true life in Jesus, will this family then say, "Paul hasn't mentioned tithing per se; maybe we can get away with only giving two percent or five percent"? Before conversion they had been giving 10 percent plus all the Temple dues, sacrifices and offerings. Now, in light of all that Christ had done for them, do you think they would be talking about how little they could give and still appear righteous?!

The church at Corinth was predominately non-Jewish, so in case they thought they could ignore the Mosaic Old Testament principles of tithing, Paul emphasized their need to excel in the grace of giving. Paul referred to the Macedonian Christians who were not wealthy, but they had not only promised to give but also kept their word in doing so (see 2 Cor. 8:1-7). He stressed that after these Macedonians had taken the collection, the money was responsibly administered and accounted for. (Any church or organization that is secret about its finances should be viewed very cautiously.)

Though they were poor, the Macedonians gave generously—a fact that must have stirred the Corinthian consciences. Paul says "out of their poverty" the Macedonians gave willingly, thankfully, lovingly and even sacrificially with great joy (see 2 Cor. 8). This reminds me of the saying, "It's not what you do with a million, if riches should be your lot, but what are you doing at present, with the $1.50 you've got." Some Christians are always making pledges and promises if they should become rich. It is a bit like the farmer who never sows seed saying if somehow he should reap a harvest, then one day he will sow some seed. If you want a harvest, you have to plant seed!

# HISTORICAL BACKGROUND

Paul devoted two entire chapters (8 and 9) in 2 Corinthians to talk to the church in Corinth about money and how they should handle their finances.

A severe famine had struck Jerusalem and Judea, inflicting great hardship and suffering upon the Christians. Sadly, the Corinthian church, which was by no means poor, had made promises a year before to help support their brethren but had failed to do so (see 2 Cor. 8:10-12). The Corinthians were too busy taking out expensive lawsuits against one another (see 1 Cor. 6:1-11) and indulging in feasts and festivities during communion, while ignoring the poor believers among them (see 1 Cor. 11:17-22).

The Corinthians had hit a spiritual low—their giving had plummeted and they had broken their promises. Paul not only called them to task but also made them realize that by their withholding, *they* were the biggest losers: "Whoever sows sparingly will also reap sparingly, and whoever sows generously will also reap generously" (2 Cor. 9:6).

Giving to God is not some kind of heavenly income tax. We have to break free from the mentality that says the church offering is how God gets money from His people. Contemplate that for a moment. Imagine a God who owns *everything* needing what *we* can give Him. Paul taught that as we give we are sowing seed that will bring a comparable harvest into our lives.

As with natural seed, there is often a time delay before harvest takes place. But if you keep sowing, you will keep harvesting. God provides the seed and watches to see what we do with it before more is given. Will we hoard it or give it away? Those who are greedy and covetous will never be able to receive God's abundance, and God's abundance will never make

**WE ARE ONLY ABLE TO RECEIVE WHEN OUR HANDS AND HEARTS ARE OPEN TO GIVE.**

us greedy because it is only as we freely give that we can freely receive.

We are only in a place to receive when our hands and hearts are open to give. How we sow will determine how we reap. What we sow does not leave our life when we plant it. It merely moves from our present into our future. It goes ahead of us to rearrange the circumstances and meet the needs of tomorrow (see 2 Cor. 9:6).

# FAITH AND PROSPERITY TEACHINGS

With every biblical truth the greatest danger is not its denial but its distortion. What has often happened regarding the principle of giving is sadly a classic example of distorted truth.

There are those who through their teaching have been used by God to bring great healing and blessing into people's lives, but many of these same teachers have also created much controversy and heartache by emphasizing one aspect of Scripture to the neglect of others. When Satan tempted Jesus with power, possessions and prestige, when even Scripture was used to coerce Him, Jesus said, "Man shall not live by bread alone, but by every word that proceeds from the mouth of God" (Matt. 4:4, *NKJV*). Biblical balance is a fullness of truth that saves us from the danger of taking a text and turning it into a man-based technique.

Take for example what you have just read about the principle of sowing and reaping. This is a biblical teaching, but when it is used as a formula to raise funds and promote a ministry, it can easily transform giving from an attitude of worship into an act of works. We do reap what we sow. If we sow sparingly, we reap sparingly; if we sow generously, we reap generously. But this does not mean we can use mathematical formulas and spiritual equations to work out what we will get! God's generosity is seen not only in what He gives but also in what He withholds. I thank Him for the prayers He has answered and especially for some He did not answer!

God knows how much He can trust us with. My 11-year-old daughter cannot wait until she has a car and passes her driving test. I suppose I could get her a car now or let her drive mine, but I love her too much. Now is not the time; she has some growing up to do first.

Over the years God has dealt with me and softened my attitude toward some of the "faith" and "prosperity" teachings and theology. The strongest criticism leveled at these movements has to do with an emphasis on money and wealth over spiritual elements of the faith. Yet many of these ministries are at least trying to take Jesus' promises seriously and not ignore or explain them away, which often happens in churches. The blessing of God is upon many of these ministries that are urging people to increase their faith and believe God for His active work in every part of their lives. Many of these faith-oriented churches see God's miraculous power in healing and provision, and many Christians testify about how their lives have been wonderfully transformed by such teaching and ministry.

Blessing, however, is not an infallible sign of theological correctness. Where would any ministry be if God only blessed us when we got it 100 percent right all the time? While theology is very important, God also looks at the heart. He often blesses people not because of the sermon, but in spite of it. Skewed teaching must never become an excuse for an "anything goes" attitude; rather, it is an acknowledgment of the grace of God and His desire to bless even when preachers do not always get it right.

God blesses some ministries not for their absolute biblical accuracy or theological astuteness but because they help to move people in the right direction. Their theology on healing may not be perfect, but they help move people toward a God who is the great Healer. Their teachings on finances may be unbalanced, but they help people understand that God is a great provider. Their teachings on faith may not always be accurate, but they direct people toward a God who rewards those who earnestly seek Him and who understand that without faith it is impossible to please Him (see Heb. 11:6).

Such teaching emphasizes expectant faith, which is very important in experiencing God's reward and provision. We are told in Hebrews 3 that those who came out of Egypt and had God's promises died in the wilderness because they did not mix faith with what they heard. We can give generously and regularly and it can become just a duty or routine. We sow seed but do not plant it with expectant faith, and then we wonder why there is no harvest. As we give tithes and offerings, it needs to be with the trust and anticipation that God will multiply back into our lives what we sow. Our belief must be that He will meet our every need and that in Him there is *always* enough.

But when does expectant faith become presumptuous force, theological error or biblical inaccuracy? This is where so much confusion arises. Jesus taught a great deal about the importance and power of expectant faith. But He also rebuked the devil's challenge to throw Himself off the Temple and let God's angels lift Him up (see Luke 4:9-12). Satan misused a passage from Psalm 91 to try and coerce Jesus, but the Lord would not presume on that because His relationship with the Father gave Him a peace and understanding of what was God's will for His life.

Expectant faith comes with the Word of God or in the promises of God, quickened by the Holy Spirit into our lives. It is the fellowship of faith—not the force of faith—that we need in order to grow in our walk with God. The truth that sets us free is a person, not a principle. The Christian life is not governed by rules and techniques; it is about relationship and trust: "The just shall live by faith" (Rom. 1:17, *KJV*).

So is it wrong to give in order to get something back from God? Yes and no. Man looks at the outward, but God sees the heart. We should give because God commands it; giving expresses our desire to put Him first and foremost in our lives. We should not give just to get something in return, for this violates giving as an act of love. God does tell us to trust Him and prove Him, as He promises to give bountiful blessings to those who obey His commands.

If our giving is only driven by what we can get back, then we can become guilty of treating God like the stock market; do not be surprised if your shares crash. God will not feed our greed or materialism, but He will meet our needs and make us a blessing to others.

This truth about faithful living is true for all time, for all people and in all places. A question worth pondering is, Why do some ministries only seem to excel in the wealthier nations of the world? Would they have reached such prominence if they were based in the Third World?

# GIVING IN THE LIGHT OF WHAT GOD GIVES TO US

You know the grace of our Lord Jesus Christ, that though He was rich, yet for your sakes He became poor, so that you through His poverty might become rich (2 Cor. 8:9).

We must always interpret a biblical text within its context; otherwise it can become a pretext for anything we want it to say.

Many a good sermon has been preached on this verse, which gives a call to deeper commitment to Christ. This is rightly so, because the context concerns God's giving to us and what should be our giving to Him. Yet it is even more specific than this because Paul was speaking primarily about the giving of money.

Some use this verse to try to prove that God wants us to be financially rich. They say Jesus did not become poor through a diminishing of His deity, "for in Him dwells all the fullness of the Godhead bodily" (Col. 2:9, *NKJV*). Some teachers point to the context in which Paul was speaking concerning the giving of finances, concluding that Jesus became poor financially so that we may become rich materially.

This provokes an immediate reaction from those who say such teaching demeans what Christ came to do. They claim it is a gospel of materialistic selfishness that is counter to what the Cross stands for. After all, it is argued, if Jesus became poor financially, why should we aim to become materially wealthy and financially rich? Surely Jesus should be our example in all things!

Theological and emotional battle lines are drawn with some making financial prosperity a sign of God's blessing and others making poverty the seal of His favor. Material prosperity can easily mean spiritual poverty for the empty-hearted, selfish individual, while spiritual prosperity can coexist with material poverty (e.g., Mother Teresa). One's spiritual wealth has little to do with material fortune. When you measure by Kingdom values, poverty and prosperity are about your *quality of life*.

It seems to me, according to both the context here and what Scripture says elsewhere, that there is a social and spiritual dimension to what Jesus gave up when He was born into this world. His birth took place amidst very humble circumstances, and He lived His early life like a fugitive, shuttling between Bethlehem, Egypt and Nazareth to escape Herod's murderous plots against the Messianic king. There is little mention of Joseph during Jesus' ministry, indicating that he had probably died some time between Jesus' twelfth and thirtieth years. This would have placed the responsibility upon Jesus, as the eldest son, to provide for His family.

There are those who argue that Jesus was rich. They state that He wore a seamless robe (a most expensive garment), probably had His own home in Capernaum, retained a treasurer to look after His finances and so forth. This point of view, however, must be understood in light of the fact that His needs were met in order to release Him to minister freely. But He certainly was not prosperous, as the world understands the word. He had to borrow someone else's boat, ride on someone else's donkey and was dependent upon others' hospitality and the support of a few godly women. When He was crucified, His possessions did not amount to much—He was even buried in another man's tomb.

There is also a spiritual aspect to Jesus becoming poor. According to Philippians 2:5-11, He voluntarily gave up the glory He once knew with the Father (see John 17:1,2). This does not mean that the Son of God's intrinsic deity was lessened, but rather in the incarnation of Jesus there came a self-limiting of His eternal fullness.

Jesus did not suffer upon the cross to make us all millionaires. His sacrifice, however, was sufficient to meet our every need, including our financial necessities. Real prosperity is not defined by having a million dollars in the bank, especially when you are unable to sleep because of worry and stress. Actually, you can prosper with no money in the bank, enjoying a good night's sleep because you know that the Lord is your shepherd and you shall not want. In other words, it all comes back to how you define riches and prosperity. I do so in the words of Paul: "Every need met" (see Phil. 4:19). True riches are found in true surrender and peace in God—in a condition of spiritual fullness.

But how do we define need? One man's need is another man's greed. This we must leave to God, for there are times when we may think our needs are not being met. The call is not to seek the meeting of the need but to seek God, who is the Giver, and place our trust in Him.

*Notes*
1. William Barclay, *The Daily Study Bible: The Revelation of John*, vol. 2 (Edinburgh: Saint Andrews Press, 1976), p. 156
2. Ibid., pp. 156, 157.
3. Tom Rees, *Money Talks* (London: Billing and Sons Ltd., 1963), p. 33.
4. Ibid.

# CHAPTER 4

# MONEY, DEBT AND GOD'S WORD

*Money has demonically usurped the role in modern society which*
*the Holy Spirit is to have in the Church.*

THOMAS MERTON

What is money, anyway? And why has it gained such critical importance in the world? As we have mentioned, Christ thought the subject so important that He spoke about it more than heaven. In this chapter we will explore the origins of money and how it has come to hold such influence over our lives and motives.

## THE BIRTH OF MONEY

How did the use of money begin? As far back as history is recorded, money has always been used. Some historians argue that in ancient societies money was not used for everyday trade. Instead,

currency was used only for certain ceremonial and public trans-
fers, such as tribute, bride price and blood money. As economies
developed, money was used more and more for ordinary trade.

Early currencies tended to consist of metals, although
cowries (shells) were used for a long time in Africa. Coinage was
probably invented in ancient China around 700 B.C. and was
subsequently reinvented by the Lydians in what is modern-day
Turkey. Paper currency also began in China, as early as the
eleventh century. We also know that ancient Babylon had a highly developed monetary system with banks and credit, as did
ancient Greece and Rome.

For reasons not fully known and understood, during the
early centuries A.D. in Europe, the money economy went into a
decline and the barter system re-emerged. During the ninth century, however, the European economy started to monetize again.

Simply defined, money is a standard of value for goods
received and services rendered. Money is anything people will
accept in exchange for goods or services, in the belief that they
may in turn exchange it later for other goods or services.

Expressions used to talk about money, such as "shell out,"
"paying a fee" and "not worth his salt," have a fascinating background. The words "shell out" date back to the time when shells
were used for money. The use of ornamental shells as money
spread from China and India eastward to the islands of the
Pacific Ocean. Such shells were used as a medium of exchange as
far away as parts of Africa and even the Americas.

The expression "paying a fee" has its origin in Germany.
There the word for cattle is *Vieh*, pronounced "fee." Long ago, if
a farmer wished to pay his debt to his local doctor or landlord,
he would take along one of his cows.

The phrase "not worth his salt" goes back to the days of the
Roman Empire. Salt was a very scarce commodity because a way

had not yet been discovered to extract it in large quantities from the earth or sea. Roman soldiers were paid a *salarium*, or "salt money," and it is from that Latin word that we derive the word "salary."

The first dollar was coined by the counts of Schlik in 1519. It was called a *Joachimsthaler* after Joachimsthal, the place in Bohemia where silver was mined for the coins. The name was too long, and eventually it became shortened to *Thaler*, the name changing phonetically according to the language of the country in which it was circulated. When the Germans officially authorized the coin, it was called the *Reichsthaler*. In Scandinavia, it became known as the *rijksdaalder*, and in Poland it was simply the *taler*. Later in the eighteenth century, it became known in America as the dollar.[1]

# MONEY IN AMERICA

When the early settlers came to America, they brought with them quite a variety of currencies from the countries they had left behind. Naturally, their paper money was only as good as the integrity of those who used it. The value of that money rose or fell in proportion to the financial strength of the institution underwriting the paper currency. In colonial America, the lines of communication were circuitous and often interrupted. News traveled slowly—by ship, by horse or on foot. Sometimes colonists found themselves possessing paper currencies of supposed value, only to learn later they were virtually worthless.

In an effort to alleviate this problem, pioneers petitioned the British government in the 1700s for the privilege of creating their own currency. The petition was denied by King George III of England. This denial of the colonists' right to print their own money became a major contributing factor to their demand for independence. Benjamin Franklin said, "We would gladly have borne the tax on tea if we could have been granted the power to create our own money."[2]

When the American colonists were short of money, they would use almost anything as a medium of exchange—whiskey, beaver skins, musket balls, corn, tobacco, cattle. It was all legal tender. With the winning of the War of Independence and the peace signing in 1783, the new nation was free to create its own money. But the newly formed United States of America had a serious problem as there was not enough gold in their reserves to represent sufficient backing for their paper currency. In some states like Virginia, Maryland and North Carolina, tobacco was adopted as a money standard and became legal tender. When the price of tobacco rose or fell, the value of the paper money rose and fell accordingly.

## KEYNESIAN ECONOMICS

The name John Maynard Keynes is today unfamiliar to most, but this man's economic beliefs continue to influence and affect our lives more than we imagine. Keynesian economics teaches that the government is the final resource: Government can answer every problem and create something out of nothing— namely, prosperity. This economic philosophy is the prevailing thought that drives many of the world's economies today. It is both fascinating and frightening how such a concept gained control in monetary policy.

This philosophy clearly paves the way for what the Bible says will happen regarding a world leader and moneyless system in the last days (see Rev. 13:7,16,17). It was President Garfield who said in 1881, "He who controls the money of the nation, controls the nation." Meyer Amschel Rothschild, one of the founders of the Rothschild banking dynasty, put it like this: "Give me control over a nation's economy, and I care not who writes its laws."

Keynes was a well-bred Englishman born in 1883. In the early years of his education, Keynes demonstrated himself to be intellectually brilliant and convincing. By the age of 14, he had won a scholarship to Eton, where he enjoyed great success as a student before going on to King's College at Cambridge. By 1907, Keynes found himself in the India Office in the service of his government.

As World War I drew near, Keynes was called by the British government to the treasury and given the assignment of working on the overseas finances of Britain. In this position he was soon dealing in the currencies of Spain, Germany, France, Italy, the United States and others. Once in the midst of such a swirl of economic instruments, he could not help but develop awareness, convictions and theories as to what might be done with those unstable things called national currencies. Soon he became an important figure in the British treasury. Many thought that he contributed more in his post to the winning of the war than did any other person in civilian life.

The crash of the American stock market on Black Tuesday in October 1929 is still thought of as the most memorable day in the economic history of civilization. The euphoric belief in continuing prosperity and growth was dealt a fatal blow that day. Millions of people who had gone into debt to invest in the stock market lost all they had. Since that infamous day, anything that has had to do with money or investments has been more carefully watched, more judiciously handled.

Understandably, everyone asked, "How did it happen? What went wrong? How could it have been avoided? What can we do to restructure it all? Is there a tie-in between economics and politics?" Still, no answers seemed to be forthcoming and the West moved into the gray, cheerless years of the Great Depression.

This was the economic atmosphere into which John Maynard Keynes stepped and was hailed as a savior. Keynes thought he had proven that government intervention would move the economy. According to his theories, government guarantees would stabilize the banks; government protection would satisfy the labor unions; and government regulation would stabilize transportation, travel, the media, housing, mortgages, pension funds and retirement plans.

That assumption allowed Keynes to produce immediate, satisfying short-term solutions. Someone is reported to have asked Keynes, "Yes, this appears to work in the short term, but what about the long-term consequences?" Keynes's famous answer: "In the long term, we are all dead." But what about future generations?

In his book *The Keynesian Revolution*, Lawrence R. Klein wrote regarding national debt, "An internally held public debt can never be a burden because we owe it to ourselves." Franklin Roosevelt echoed the same feelings: "Our national debt, after all, is an internal debt, owed not only by the nation but to the nation. If our children have to pay the interest, they will have to pay it to themselves."[3]

The problem with this philosophy is that the wealth of the nation gets channeled and funneled into the hands of a smaller and smaller minority of people. In 1982, the U.S. national debt was equal to 36 percent of the gross domestic product (GDP). In 1991, the national debt had risen to 64 percent of the GDP. Today it is over $3 *trillion*! The debt is growing faster than the economy.

# THE POWER OF INTEREST

In his book *The Chronology of Money,* Wickcliffe B. Vennard illustrates the power of compound interest by showing how if one penny were invested in A.D. 1 at 6 percent compounded interest, by 1895 that penny would have accrued to a value of $8,497,840 decillion! This is more than all the wealth in the world combined a million times over.[4]

Thomas Jefferson wrote, "The question whether one generation has the right to bind another by the deficit it imposes is a question of such consequence as to place it among the fundamental principles of government. We should consider ourselves unauthorized to saddle posterity with our debts, and morally bound to pay them ourselves."

Keynesian economics has created an environment where there will need to come a financial savior. This counterfeit savior, I believe, will come in the form of the antichrist spoken of in Revelation. In the final chapter of this book, we will examine what the Bible says about the end times, the economy and God's ultimate plan.

The debt mentality is one of negativity and loss—whether that debt is incurred on a national level or a personal level. It is part and parcel of the Never Enough Syndrome that grabs for today but does not think about others (i.e., our posterity). But how did debt begin, and what does the Bible have to say about it?

# THE HISTORY OF DEBT

The Bible allows lending and borrowing within the boundaries of justice and compassion. Israelites could lend to fellow Israelites, but they could only keep a pledge of payment so long as it did not cause harm to the poor person, and they were forbidden to charge interest (see Exod. 22:25-27).

The Israelites were commanded to lend generously to the poor and not be tightfisted against them, even if it looked like the poor might not be able to pay them back (see Deut. 15:7-10). Israelites were to treat other Israelites as members of a faith community, and they were not to take advantage of people in desperate circumstances (see Neh. 5:1-11). On the other hand, lending at interest to non-Israelites was allowed (see Deut. 23:19-20).

For the first 12 centuries A.D., lending money at interest was strictly and repeatedly forbidden by the councils of the Church. The prohibition was based upon the theory that money was solely for the purpose of exchanging goods, the return of an equal amount of value—charging interest would have been unequal and unfair overpayment. In A.D. 901, King Alfred the Great of England declared, "If any man is found taking usury, his lands will be confiscated and he will be banished from England." In 1215, King John echoed this pronouncement, and as late as 1566, King James I stated, "Usury . . . is taking a man's life and it must not be tolerated."[5]

Today, money is no longer seen merely as a medium of exchange but as a resource capable of producing wealth just like other property. From the sixteenth to the eighteenth centuries, Christian churches gradually relaxed the absolute prohibition against interest. Since then, the Christian Church has tolerated exaction of a reasonable interest for a loan, and the term "usury" has tended to imply excessive rates.[6]

We can see then from the Bible and from the evolution of the understanding of usury that incurring interest-bearing debts is not *always* wrong. However, there is something wrong if we continually allow our expenses to outpace our income and we enter into a lifestyle of debt.

Consumer debt is debt incurred to purchase "consumable" goods and services (e.g., cars, clothes and airfares). Consumer debt is much different from mortgage debt or business debt. Mortgage debt makes it possible for people who do not have hundreds of thousands of dollars on hand to purchase a home. If the market for homes in an area is good, mortgage debt may even be a way of increasing wealth as property values increase.

Business debt is an investment that aims to increase wealth through producing something new that people want to buy (e.g., a start-up business), or to increase productivity for an existing business. Mortgage debts and business debts are usually financed over longer periods at less expensive interest rates than consumer debts.

In the next chapter we will look at ways we can break out of the world's money-centered mind-set and gain power over our finances.

*Notes*

1. Willard Cantalon, *The Day the Dollar Dies* (New Jersey: Logos International, 1973), pp. 39-41.
2. Ibid., p. 41.
3. Ibid., p. 33.
4. Ibid., p. 32.
5. Ibid.
6. The Councils of Arles (A.D. 314), Nicaea (325), Carthage (348), Aix (789), the Third Lateran Council (1179), the Second Council of Lyons (1274), Thomas Aquinas, Pope Benedict (1745), Martin Luther, Ulrich Zwingli and other sixteenth-century Anglican church leaders all forbade interest (usury). John Calvin allowed it. England allowed it in 1571, and Germany and the other European countries eventually followed. See the article on usury in the *Oxford Dictionary of the Christian Church,* edited by F. L. Cross and E. A. Livingstone (Oxford University Press, 1958, 1983), p. 1420.

# CHAPTER 5

# GAINING POWER OVER MONEY

*Money will buy you a bed but not sleep. Books but not brains. Food but not appetite. Medicine but not health. Luxury but not culture. Amusement but not happiness. A crucifix but not a Savior.[1]*

The Jews have a saying: "Whosoever craves wealth is like a man who drinks seawater. The more he drinks the more he thirsts, and he continues to drink until he perishes."

Biblically, material wealth is embodied by such things as land, cattle, flocks, property, silver and gold. Wealth can be defined as all that God has created, and He claims ownership (see Ps. 24:1). Money, on the other hand, is a human invention.

In Matthew 22:17-21, Jesus asks for a coin and is given a Roman denarius, the only coin that could be used to pay the hated yearly poll tax. He asks those present whose face is on the coin, knowing already that it bears the image of Emperor Tiberius. Around the edge of the coin are written the words "Tiberius Caesar

Augustus, son of the divine Augustus." On the reverse side of the coin, where Tiberius's mother is represented as the goddess of peace, there appear words that command the worship of Caesar.

When Jesus declares, "Render to Caesar what belongs to Caesar and render to God what belongs to God" (Matt. 22:21), He was asserting that when man takes what belongs to God and places on it his own image, it becomes damaging and destructive to those who crave it.

If we do not take control of our money, it will take control of us. Whether you have control over money or it has control over you depends upon your attitude toward it and your actions with it. It was Nobel Peace Prize winner Albert Schweitzer, doctor and missionary to Africa, who said, "If there is something you own that you can't give away, you don't own it—it owns you."[2] If this is true, then how do we gain power over our money?

# GUARD YOUR HEART

When God measures a man He puts the tape around his heart and not his head. — Scottish Proverb

The first U.S. coin to bear the inscription "In God We Trust" was a two-cent piece minted in 1864. The idea for the inscription originated with a Pennsylvania minister who suggested it to Salmon Portland Chase, Secretary of the Treasury under Abraham Lincoln. Chase, a deeply God-fearing man, asked the director of the mint, James Polloch, to come up with appropriate words. In a letter to Polloch, Chase wrote, "No nation can be strong except in the strength of God, or safe except in His defense. The trust of our people in God should be declared on our national coins."

So the motto "In God We Trust" was born. It is one thing to inscribe these words on our currency; it is life changing when it is written on our hearts.

Worldliness is not defined by the amount of our possessions but by the attitude of our hearts toward them. "Above all else, guard your heart, for it is the wellspring of life" (Prov. 4:23). The first time God called for an offering from the Israelites He emphasized that true giving, the giving that He would bless, came from the heart. "Tell the Israelites to bring me an offering. You are to receive the offering for me from each man whose heart prompts him to give" (Exod. 25:2).

The Early Church at Jerusalem exhibited amazing generosity and love because God had changed their hearts. Acts 4:32 says, "All the believers were one in heart and mind. No one claimed that any of his possessions was his own, but they shared everything they had."

God struck Ananias and Sapphira dead, not because they gave less, but because they misrepresented what they gave as the whole price. The apostle Peter confronted them with their lie:

> How is it that Satan has so filled your heart that you have lied to the Holy Spirit and have kept for yourself some of the money you received for the land? Didn't it belong to you before it was sold? And after it was sold, wasn't the money at your disposal? What made you think of doing such a thing? You have not lied to men but to God (Acts 5:3,4).

Paul said, "Each man should give what he has decided in his heart to give, not reluctantly or under compulsion, for God loves a cheerful giver" (2 Cor. 9:7).

Jesus condemned the Pharisees because the way they gave revealed the true state of their hearts: "So when you give to the needy, do not announce it with trumpets, as the hypocrites do in the synagogues and on the streets, to be honored by men . . . they have received their reward in full" (Matt. 6:2).

The word "hypocrite" comes from the word *hupokrites*, a word used in Greek theater. If you have ever been to an older theater, you may have seen two masks mounted above the stage. One has a big smile and represents comedy, while the other has a big frown and represents tragedy. In the Greek world, if the scene was a tragedy, an actor would put the frowning mask over his face, so the audience could see it was a tragedy. He would put the smiling mask on to show everyone when they were enacting a comedy. The person who spoke from behind the mask was called a hypocrite. The word literally means to speak from behind the mask. God hates hypocrisy and looks to see what is in our hearts—not just our hands—when we give.

# OVERCOMING DEBT

One of life's hardest jobs is to keep up the easy payments.

In the last chapter we learned what the Bible says about debt, and how the Church's view of lending has changed through the centuries. But what does that have to do with how we live today? It seems that debt, for our culture, is here to stay. Consider the following statistics as proof.

More than 266,000 Americans filed for bankruptcy during the first three months of 1996. By the end of that year more than one million individuals went bankrupt. At the time of this writing, one American household in every hundred is in a state of bankruptcy. Household debt in the U.S. has reached an all-time high of more than $1.14 trillion—as much as Great Britain's entire gross domestic product.[3]

In our society, it is almost impossible to avoid some kind of debt at one time or another. Whether the debt is incurred for a house, car, personal business or washing machine, debt for many is a fact of life. In Romans 13:8 we read, "Let no debt remain outstanding, except the continuing debt to love one another." Does this mean that Christians should never enter into financial debt? Some believe it does. Hudson Taylor, who founded the China Inland Mission, would never incur a debt, basing his conviction on this verse. Charles Spurgeon likewise held to the same conviction.

I believe that avoiding *all* debt stretches Romans 13:8 too far. As we discussed in the last chapter, the Bible does not forbid borrowing or legal financial transactions that involve interest. What the Bible does forbid is the charging of high interest, robbing the brethren and failing to pay honest debts (see Exod. 22:25-27; Neh. 5:1-11). Paul's instruction was to continue to love one another; this is a debt from which we will never be free.

Whereas I do not believe it is wrong for Christians to have a debt, there is something seriously wrong if we make debt a habit and our debt ends up having *us*. We must be alert and avoid a situation where our expenses outpace our income and we enter into a lifestyle of debt.

Unwise accumulation of consumer debt can be devastating to individuals and families. In 1982 the amount of monthly income used to pay consumer debt in America averaged 16 percent. By 1996 this had risen to 29.5 percent.[4] The average amount of credit card debt per U.S. cardholder is more than $4,000.[5] A credit card can be a good servant, but it has the potential to become a vicious master. Banks in the United States have commissioned studies that showed if a person uses a credit card for purchases, he or she will spend on average 34 percent more per year than if they paid for transactions only in cash.[6]

Let me ask a question: Do you own a credit card, or does a credit card own you? If you find that you cannot live without your card because you need credit to help finance your debts, then radical action is necessary before you enter the debt spiral. May I suggest a little plastic surgery? Consider cutting up the card.

How do you overcome the power of debt? First, recognize that you may have a problem—a proper diagnosis is required for a lasting cure. Then, ask for God's guidance and the help of others you trust who are skilled in debt management. Work with them to develop a strategy to help you win your battle over debt. Realize that you probably sank into this problem over a long period of time. The long-term answer is not a divine crisis bailout but a series of lifestyle changes that will help you take back the ground that debt has occupied in your life.

If God reveals that you need to repent about certain decisions and behaviors, then repent and ask His forgiveness. If you feel life has backed you into a debt spiral that is really not your fault, then forgive those who have wronged you. Refuse to be bitter and seek God for the way ahead, knowing that He loves you and desires what is best for your life.

# THE BLESSING OF A BUDGET

If your outgoings exceed your income, your upkeep will be your downfall.

In Charles Dickens's *David Copperfield*, Mr. Micawber gives a very true-to-life analysis of economics when he says, "Annual income £20, annual expenditure £19, 19 shillings and sixpence.

Result: happiness. Annual income £20, annual expenditure £20 and sixpence. Result: misery."

Financial problems are among the most common sources of stress for young families. Men and women often see the importance of money from different viewpoints. The woman's greater need is for security and the man's is for significance. These differences often result in clashes over how the family uses its income. Agreeing to a sensible budget will go a long way in helping to sort out any problems that may arise.

We need to both plan and trust in God for our provision, being wise in how we save and spend. We should continually evaluate our current finances and ask, "Where is our money going? Are we living within our means?" This will help you avoid living on the edge all the time. It will also help you set aside a little bit for investing, so that sudden needs do not bring total panic. A good budget reflects the truth that we are not to be skinflints or spendthrifts but good stewards of all that God has given us.

A budget is like a theological document: It shows who or what we worship.

# PRAY ABOUT YOUR USE OF MONEY

The care of $200 million is too great a load for any brain or back to bear. It is enough to ill anyone. There is no pleasure in it. — W. H. Vanderbilt

If you suddenly inherit a large sum of money, the first thing to do after expressing your joy is to pray. Sudden wealth has been the ruin of many a life and family. In prayer we are able to confess our greed and ask for God's help in being a good steward of

His resources. God will speak to us in prayer and guide us to freedom from the bondage that money and possessions can have over us.

We must not make the mistake of thinking that if we give God our tithes and offerings, we can do what we like with the rest. *Everything* we have belongs to God. Tithes and offerings are given to acknowledge that we put God first, but if we spend the rest regardless of Him, then we contradict our very act of giving. If living is a constant struggle and anxiety despite the fact that we tithe, then the problem may be that we are not seeking to honor God in what we should be doing with the rest of our income.

The Bible tells us that the whole world is in the hands of the evil one (see 1 John 5:19). Satan is the god of this age (see 2 Cor. 4:4) and the prince of the power of the air (see Eph. 2:2). When the Bible speaks of the world, it is referring to the world's way of thinking and living, which is almost always counter to God's way of doing things. This world's lifestyle is not controlled by the fashion houses of Paris or the media industry of Hollywood or the latest philosophical idea. Rather, the world is governed by spiritual powers of darkness and wickedness that operate behind the world's systems and values (see Eph. 6:12; Rom. 12:2). Satan still offers the kingdoms of this world to destroy and devour his victims.

It is through prayer that we are able to do the following:

- Pull down financial and worldly strongholds that the enemy seeks to build in our lives
- Perceive whether or not the power and lust for money has found its way into our souls
- Ask God to lead us not into temptation but deliver us from the evil one

• Position our lives to be channels for God's blessing to others

# KEEP IN TOUCH WITH THE POOR

When you help the poor, you are lending to the Lord and he pays wonderful interest on your loan (see Prov. 19:17).

There is a story told of a poor Irish beggar living on the streets of New York City. It was the morning of the annual Saint Patrick's Day parade and the beggar was asking for money along Fifth Avenue. As a couple strolled by he called out, "May the blessing of the Lord, which brings love and joy and wealth and a fine family, follow you all the days of your life!" The couple arrogantly ignored the beggar as they passed his outstretched hand. Then he shouted after them, "And never catch up to you!"

Our attitude toward the poor is a great revealer of our hearts. God hates injustice and condemns inequality. The provision of the Year of Jubilee in Israel's community life had tremendous social and spiritual significance (see Lev. 25:9-54). Every 50th year all land and property were returned to their original Jewish owners, and every Hebrew slave would be set free unless the slave chose to stay and continue serving his master. In Luke 4:18,19, Jesus touched on social welfare as He read from Isaiah:

The Spirit of the Lord is on me, because he has anointed me to preach good news to the poor. He has sent me to proclaim freedom for the prisoners and recovery of sight for the blind, to release the oppressed, to proclaim the year of the Lord's favor.

Not only was Jesus revealing the dynamic of healing and deliverance within His ministry, but He was also emphasizing the dimension of social welfare. God's concern for the poor is one of the most important and prominent themes in the Bible.

When most Christians are asked what was the greatest evil of Sodom, they invariably mention sexual sin. But they fail to remember how the prophet Ezekiel condemned Sodom's sin:

> Now this was the sin of your sister Sodom: She and her daughters were arrogant, overfed and unconcerned; they did not help the poor and needy. They were haughty and did detestable things before me. Therefore I did away with them as you have seen (Ezek. 16:49,50).

While statistics can never tell the whole story, they do help reveal what the big picture really looks like. Each day 40,000 children die of hunger and preventable diseases.[7] The World Bank estimates that almost one person in four in our world—a staggering 1.3 billion—lives in grinding poverty, struggling to survive, living on a mere $1 a day. About 1.5 billion have no access to health services, and 1.3 billion lack safe drinking water. According to the United Nations, it would cost approximately 30 to 40 billion dollars a year to provide all people in developing countries with basic education, health care and clean water—the same amount that is spent on golf every year. This is not a reflection on the game of golf, but it is an indicator of the huge gulf that exists between the rich and poor.[8]

According to the *United Nations 1996 Human Development Report*, the combined wealth of the world's 358 billionaires now equals the total income of the poorest 45 percent of the world's population. The richest 20 percent of the world's population—which includes the vast majority of Christians in Western nations—is 150 times as rich as the poorest 20 percent.[9] This abundance makes generous giving and sharing not only possible but also commanded by God. Yet the richer we become, the less we give.

Mother Teresa was admired and applauded for her work. She said, "I have found the paradox that if I love until it hurts, then there is no hurt but only more love."[10] The diminutive nun was awarded the Nobel Peace Prize for her labor of love to the poor and destitute on the streets of Calcutta and around the world. She made a very telling statement that we would all do well to stop and ponder: "Today, talking about the poor is in fashion. Knowing, loving and serving the poor is quite a different matter."

The typical American family is twice as wealthy as in 1957. Church giving, however, has declined almost every year since 1968, when the typical church member gave about one-third of a biblical tithe (i.e., 3.14 percent of their income). By 1995, the typical church member gave less than a quarter of a tithe (2.46 percent of their income). We are spending more and more on ourselves and less and less on others.[11]

A popular adaptation of Jesus' charge to care for the poor and downtrodden (see Matt. 25:34-46) puts it like this: "I was hungry and you formed a committee to investigate my hunger. I was homeless and you filed a report. I was sick and you held a seminar on the situation of the underprivileged. You have investigated all aspects of my plight and I am still hungry, homeless and sick."

This tendency is reflected in the results of an experiment carried out by a small group of seminary students involving their classmates. The class was given an assignment on Luke 10:33-37, the story of the Good Samaritan. The classmates were given very little time—the assignment was to be handed in promptly the next day or they would lose marks. The following morning, one of the students disguised himself in old clothes and makeup that made him appear badly beaten and bruised. He placed himself on the path that his fellow classmates would travel on their way to class, their assignments in hand. Not even one student stopped or paused to help. Everyone was too busy and concerned about getting his or her assignment in on time to recognize the priority of the situation. They chose grades over compassion.

Remembering and helping the poor helps us to keep our hearts and priorities right. When we are tempted to complain about our lack, it is very humbling to be made aware of those who have much less. There is an old proverb that says, "I complained I had no shoes until I met a man who had no feet."

William Booth, in founding the Salvation Army, never lost sight of what God had called him to do. God clearly called him to preach the gospel and reach out to the poor and downtrodden of society. Despite hostile opposition from

**AN OLD PROVERB SAYS, "I COMPLAINED I HAD NO SHOES UNTIL I MET A MAN WHO HAD NO FEET."**

both inside and outside the Church, his ministry grew to become admired all over the world.

When the British government sought to reward war hero General Charles George Gordon for his brilliant service in the Chinese Uprising (1860–1865), he declined all money and titles but accepted a gold medal inscribed with the record of his 33 engagements. It was his most prized possession. After his death in 1885, the medal could not be found. Eventually, it was learned that he had sent it to Manchester during a severe famine, directing it to be melted down and used to buy bread for the poor. Under the date of its sending, these words were found written in his diary, "The last earthly thing I had in this world that I valued I have given to the Lord Jesus Christ."[12]

General Gordon is buried in the famous St. Paul's Cathedral in London. His epitaph reads: "Sacred to the memory of Charles George Gordon who at all times and everywhere gave his strength to the weak, his substance to the poor, his sympathy to the suffering, his heart to God."

What are most important are not the possessions we have but the people we help. One traveler in Africa told how he watched a nun dressing the wounds of a leper. The flesh was rotting, smelled revolting and looked repulsive. As he watched her he said, "I wouldn't do that for ten thousand dollars." She looked up at him and said, "I wouldn't either."

A few years ago I attended a "Go to the Nations" missionary conference in Brazil. One of the most powerful speakers was a young woman named Rosealea who was training to become a missionary to the Kurds in northern Iraq. Her heart was filled with passion and compassion for these refugees who had suffered horribly at the hands of Saddam Hussein and under other brutal regimes. She told us that the Kurds were the Muslim group considered most open to the gospel. She was going into a dangerous situation, as more than 1.5 million Kurds had been forced to flee to the caves and mountains of northern Iraq to escape the chemical weapons and guns of Saddam. Unfortunately, other nations had closed their borders to the fleeing Kurds.

Rosealea described the dream of one missionary nurse already working with the Kurds. In it the nurse saw a long line of people waiting for food, which she handed out as they slowly filed past. Finally she came to the end of the line and looked up and saw Jesus. She was surprised and said, "Jesus, You are here, too?"

He replied, "That which you do unto the least of these you have done to Me."

# DEVELOP A BIBLICAL ATTITUDE

When we talk about a man's worth, we usually do so in terms of money and possessions. We say a man is worth more than $1 million, or she is worth a small fortune. When asked the question "What are they worth?" about a set of objects, the answer is commonly given in terms of dollars. This may be society's way of evaluating worth, but it is not Scripture's. A biblical attitude does not assess a person by what is in his pocket but, rather, what is in his heart.

We are warned not to show favoritism to the rich. James rebukes those who are influenced by a person's wealth or those who give the wealthy special attention while neglecting the poor. When we do this, we show our ignorance and worldliness and reveal our wrong values (see Jas. 2:1-9).

Soon after the beginning of this century, a 350-pound wrestler from Turkey won the European wrestling championship. His name was Yosef and he was known as the "Terrible

Turk." Seeking to capture the world championship title, he went to the United States and challenged the American champ at that time, Strangler Lewis.

Lewis had won the U.S. title with an unusual tactic, which also gave him his nickname. He would wrap his huge arm around his opponent's neck and press his throat until he collapsed from lack of oxygen. But the Turk's neck was so huge that Strangler Lewis could not get his arm around it. Lewis, weighing a mere 200 pounds, found that he was helpless, as his one weapon was useless. The Terrible Turk tossed him around the ring like a tennis ball and easily won the match.

Yosef gained the title and $5,000, which was his portion of the ticket sales. He demanded his payment in U.S. gold, which he crammed into a money belt and strapped around his huge waist. He set sail on a ship back to Europe, but en route the ship sank in the Atlantic. Yosef went over the side with his prize money in gold still strapped to his waist. The weight of the money belt made it impossible for him to stay afloat, and he sank like an anvil. He was a man whose life was attached to the wrong values—values that eventually killed him.

The editor of *Money* magazine made a telling comment when he said, "Money has become the new sex in this country."[13] Money is the number one obsession of Americans—and most other nations around the world.

A survey of *Discipleship Journal* readers ranked the areas that were the greatest spiritual challenge to them:

1. Materialism
2. Pride
3. Self-centeredness
4. Laziness
5. Anger/bitterness

6. Sexual lust
7. Envy
8. Gluttony
9. Lying

The survey respondents noted that temptations were more powerful when they had neglected spending time with God and when they were physically tired. Prayer, Bible study, avoiding compromising situations and being accountable to someone were cited as the most effective ways they found of overcoming temptation.[14]

Materialism is something that virtually every Christian struggles with at some level, but what makes one a materialist? It is not merely a matter of having things but, rather, the condition of being obsessed and possessed by them. A multimillionaire who lives in a mansion and drives a beautiful car is not necessarily a materialist, while a virtual pauper living in a hovel can be materialistic in everything he thinks and does. The Bible does not give us a specific formula to let us know if we have stepped over the line into materialism, but here are some of the warning signs:

## 1. POSSESSIONS HAVE BECOME MORE IMPORTANT TO YOU THAN PEOPLE

Jim Bakker was the leader of one of America's biggest Christian television ministries before being tried and found guilty of fraud and sentenced to several years in prison. He has since been released and gives his own account of what caused his downfall in his book *I Was Wrong*. In this very moving and enlightening book, Bakker says that many of his beliefs and teachings regarding money and possessions are now radically different from what he once taught.

While in jail he began to read and study again what Scripture actually taught about prosperity and the use and abuse of money. He repented and admitted he had become unbalanced and unbiblical in many of his teachings. He says— and has shown—that he is a changed man from the one whom Jerry Miller, the prosecutor at his trial, described as one "who had started out loving people and using things but ended up loving things and using people."[15]

## 2. THE MATERIAL IS MORE IMPORTANT TO YOU THAN THE SPIRITUAL

I love the story of the four men who brought their paralyzed friend to Jesus (see Mark 2:3-5). Unable to make their way through the crowd, they lowered their friend down through the roof to where Jesus was teaching. Jesus saw their faith, which brought healing and forgiveness to their bedridden friend.

Their show of faith was indeed wonderful, but first the four men had to tear the roof off. Some scholars think the house was actually Jesus' home base while in Capernaum. Jesus was not concerned with the damage to the roof, however, but with the condition of the paralytic.

For Jesus, the spiritual is always more important than the material.

## 3. YOU ARE CONSTANTLY WORRYING ABOUT MONEY RATHER THAN MANAGING IT

In Matthew 6:25-34, Jesus warns the Jews not to be like the pagans, worrying constantly about what they will eat, drink and wear. There is nothing wrong with these things in themselves, but Jesus said the "pagans run after all these things." It is the pursuit of possessions, not just the possession of things, that makes a materialist.

## 4. YOU ARE COVETOUS OF WHAT OTHERS HAVE

Do you find yourself being envious and jealous of what others have? The average American adult watches five hours of television a day and sees about 21,000 commercials a year. The message from these advertisements is typically "Buy something and do it now." The largest 100 U.S. corporations pay for about 75 percent of all commercial TV sponsorship.

Two of the Ten Commandments deal with a right attitude toward another's possessions: "Thou shalt not steal" and "Thou shalt not covet." Why do so many people spend money they do not have to buy things they do not need to impress people they do not like?

## 5. YOU ARE UNGRATEFUL FOR WHAT YOU DO HAVE

Thinking and talking about what you do not have instead of being thankful for what you do have indicates a preoccupation with the material. Do you value instant gratification over your future well-being, over what God has in store for your future?

## 6. THERE IS NO JOY IN YOUR GIVING

This is an accumulative effect—and symptom—of the other traits mentioned above. At this point, a person has walked away from God's desire that we not give "reluctantly or under compulsion." Remember, "God loves a cheerful giver" (2 Cor. 9:7).

# JESUS MUST BE LORD

He is no fool to lose what he cannot keep to gain what he cannot lose. — Jim Elliot

Hollywood film star Tom Hanks is believed to earn upward of $20 million per film. He received the Academy Award for best actor two years in a row. Yet he said his greatest fear was that "his moment of glory was fleeting. It wouldn't last. What would happen when the lights went out and the crowd went home; would anybody want him to make another movie?"

Actor Lee Marvin saw through the fleeting stardom of Hollywood fame when he said in a television interview, "There are three stages in an actor's career. The first is when the film studios say, 'Lee Marvin, who is Lee Marvin?' Suddenly fame arrives and then they exclaim, 'Lee Marvin, we want Lee Marvin!' Then the years roll by and they say, 'Lee Marvin, who is Lee Marvin?'"

Another Hollywood performer, Eddie Murphy, earns around $15 million a film. When asked about his money he said, "When I didn't have much, I didn't need much. But the more I have, the more I need; and the more I need, the more I worry." When the world watches "Entertainment Tonight" or the Academy Awards broadcast, people want to see the glamour and glitz; but behind the show biz facade there often lies emptiness, fear and despair.

A few years ago my wife, who is a journalist, did an interview with a member of a California missions team visiting our church in Scotland. His story was so good that another freelance journalist asked if he could broadcast his story on the main radio station in Scotland. This was arranged and the interview went remarkably well.

By profession this missionary was a stuntman who worked in the American film industry. In his interview, he spoke about the emptiness of the Hollywood lifestyle—that many in the film industry were insecure, fearful and searching for meaning. For this stuntman, the glamour of Tinseltown was as phony as the illusions of danger he was paid to create for the cameras. It was only when he came to know Jesus Christ that he found the joy, peace and forgiveness for which he had been searching.

We were all very excited because many Scots were going to hear what God had done in this man's life. When the interview was broadcast, however, we could not believe what the producers at Radio Scotland had done. They had removed every reference to Jesus. They cut the stuntman's entire testimony. They edited what he said about Hollywood to make it appear that it was a wonderful place, full of fun and excitement—the exact opposite of what the full interview contained. I realized again the power and perversion of the media and how they have the ability to influence radically what we hear and believe.

The world is constantly seeking to influence and control us in our attitudes toward money. If we are to avoid being sucked into its hopelessly flawed system of values, we must bring our finances under the lordship of Christ. When we do this, we break free from the world's power and control and move into God's purposes and provision.

Let me illustrate this principle using a bunch of keys. Each key represents a possession: a house, a car, a garage and so on. We give them all to Jesus, saying, "From now on, it's Your house, Your car, Your possessions."

Jesus says, "You need a home to live in; here, take care of Mine. You need a car for work; borrow Mine. But remember, they are Mine and I can call on them anytime I want."

Then one day the car breaks down and you have no money to pay for the repairs. So you come and pray, "Lord, Your car has broken down and it needs urgent repairs. I ask according to Your love and lordship for help in this situation." Then bills come in for the house, and it's a struggle to pay them. So you pray, "Lord, remember the house You asked me to look after for You? Well, it has some bills that need paying."

When Jesus is made Lord of your life and is given full ownership, He blesses and honors. But sadly, many Christians have never acknowledged Jesus' lordship over all their possessions. They go to Him when they have a financial problem and say, "The car needs fixing."

Jesus could say, "Why tell Me? It's your car. You have never acknowledged Me with this before; you have never given it to Me. But now you come with the bills?!"

There are times when the Lord is so gracious that He bails us out of our own selfishness. But He wants us to grow and mature, so sometimes there are painful lessons we bring upon ourselves. God not only wants us to know His will but also to learn His ways.

*Notes*
1. A. Naismith, *1200 More Notes, Quotes and Anecdotes* (London: Pickering and Inglis Ltd., 1975), p. 135.
2. Peter Graystone, *Ready Salted* (Milton Keynes: Scripture Union, 1998), p. 115.
3. John Greenwald, "Dead Beat and Up Beat," *Time*, Vol. 148, Num. 3 (July 8, 1996), p. 44.
4. American Bankruptcy Institute and CDB Infotek, *Chicago Tribune*, October 10, 1996.
5. Bureau of Economic Analysis, as cited in the *Chicago Tribune*, October 29, 1995.
6. *Escape from Debt*, Evangelical Alliance, p. 186.
7. *A Practical Journal for Church Leaders* (Spring 1997), p. 75.

8. Ronald Sider, "What Do We Do with Poor, Hungry People?" *Charisma and Christian Life Magazine* (December 1998), p. 58.

9. *Leadership Magazine* (Spring 1998), p. 79.

10. Hannah Ward and Jennifer Wild, *The Lion Christian Quotation Collection* (London: Lion Publishing, 1997), p. 320.

11. Ronald Sider, "What Do We Do with Poor, Hungry People?" p. 58.

12. Peter Graystone, *Ready Salted*, p. 116.

13. Steve Thurman, "Life, Liberty and the Pursuit of Just a Little More," *Evangelical Beacon* (October 1992), p. 6.

14. *Discipleship Journal* (November/December 1992), p. 6.

15. Jim Bakker, *I Was Wrong* (Nashville, TN: Thomas Nelson, 1996).

CHAPTER 6

# MONEY AND SPIRITUAL WARFARE

*No one can serve two masters. You cannot serve both God and mammon.*

MATTHEW 6:24

I live and minister in the beautiful city of Aberdeen in northeast Scotland. Aberdeen is known as the Granite City because many of its buildings are made of that stone, which is not only incredibly hard but also beautiful when it glistens in the sunlight. This is a wealthy city, the oil capital of Europe. But long before oil was discovered in the North Sea, Aberdeen flourished as a center of merchant shipping and the fishing industry. Through the centuries the waters around its coast have provided much of the city's wealth.

Situated on the top of what was once a major city-center bank building is a strange statue of a woman seated on a throne. On her left by her feet lies a lion; on her right lies a horn of plenty. She is called Ceres and is known as the goddess of plenty. She has held that place of prominence for more than a hundred years. Interestingly, she was not positioned to look out over the city but in another direction—toward the harbor, which is also the red-light district. This is of particular concern to me because she overlooks the church I pastor, which is situated less than 100 yards from the main harbor and 200 yards from the statue itself.

There are two major rivers that flow out of the nearby Grampian Mountains and into the sea at Aberdeen: the River Don and the River Dee. Ancient records provide fascinating, yet frightening, details of what is reported to have happened in one of the rivers. An old saying goes, "The bonny Don she requires none; the bloody Dee she requires three." This refers to the time when live sacrifices were made by the Celts to the Kelpees, gods of the sea, to secure their provision and protection.

It is no coincidence that one evangelist, whom God sent from Africa, had a very strange experience while visiting the city. This evangelist, whom I know personally, was led by the Holy Spirit to go and pray by the sea. While he was there, God began to show him ancient covenants and sacrifices that had been made with the "gods of the waters." He prayed for these curses to be broken. Later that night, he sensed a dark presence come against him while he was in his bedroom. This spiritual power challenged him and asked why he was disturbing these forces. When this African brother told me this story the following day, I shared with him some of the history of what had happened in the past. He had heard none of it before.

## WHY DOES DARKNESS DWELL WHERE IT DOES?

I came to Elim Pentecostal Church to be its pastor in May 1987 and was greeted by a group of 40 faithful members who had recently gone through much pain and trauma. Sadly, a previous ministry member had resigned because of moral failings. Just a short time before, the pastor of a nearby church had also resigned his position because of sexual immorality.

After I had been in the church a few years, the minister of one of the largest churches in Scotland (also close by) was sentenced to three years in prison because of sexual crimes committed against children.

I prayed for mercy for those who had fallen in sexual sin but knew it was no coincidence: All three churches ministered around the red-light district and all had been rocked in the same way. Geographically, all three were situated between the statue of the goddess of plenty on one side and the mouth of the River Dee on the other, where known occult activity had once taken place.

This was my first church as a senior pastor; I had only three years of previous experience as an assistant pastor. I remember praying one Thursday night during our prayer meeting, asking God why our church had been so small for so many years. At that time I understood little about spiritual powers and dark forces ruling over and influencing specific areas. Whereas it is unwise to be preoccupied with territorial spirits, it can be equally foolish to ignore and dismiss demonic activity altogether.

When it comes to spiritual warfare, ignorance is not bliss. The devil and his demons are not in hell (see 2 Pet. 2:4; the word "hell" here is translated from *tartarus*, gloomy dungeons to be held for judgment). The demonic operates in heavenly places (see Eph. 6:12). One day Satan and his minions will be cast into hell (see Rev. 20:10), but now they dwell in darkness wherever it is found (see Jude 6).

For the purpose of our discussion, I am not going to do an in-depth study on the subject of territorial spirits and the demonic.

Other contemporary writers have covered the subject well: Peter Wagner in *Engaging the Enemy* (Ventura, CA: Regal Books, 1991) and *Breaking Strongholds in Your City* (Ventura, CA: Regal Books, 1993); Ed Silvoso in *That None Should Perish* (Ventura, CA: Regal Books, 1994); John Dawson in *Taking Our Cities for God* (Lake Mary, FL: Creation House, 1989); and Floyd McClung in *Seeing Our Cities with the Eyes of God* (Grand Rapids, MI: Chosen Books, 1991), to name just a few.

That night after the prayer meeting God clearly spoke to me. I was unable to grasp the full implications of what He said, but the experience began to shed light on what had happened and why it had occurred. The words God spoke to my spirit were: "The area has affected the church more than the church has affected the area."

Since that night more than 11 years ago, we have prayed and fasted as we have sought God to expose and penetrate the spiritual darkness around us. The first goal of such warfare prayer is not to drive out all the principalities and powers of the area. We began by praying that whatever was at work in the community would not be at work among us, that such darkness would not again infiltrate our church and would not gain any foothold to build a stronghold among us.

It is important to remember that Satan has no power to defeat us—"He who is in you is greater than he who is in the world" (1 John 4:4, *NKJV*). Rather, it is only when we open ourselves to darkness that we give the devil an advantage over us. This is why Paul went to great lengths to warn and exhort the Ephesian church to "not give the devil a foothold" (Eph. 4:27). One of your first tasks in spiritual warfare and evangelism is to ensure that your own house is in order (see Jas. 4:1-10).

Paul's letter to the Ephesians is clear about our battle against the demonic:

For our struggle is not against flesh and blood, but against
the rulers, against the authorities, against the powers of
this dark world and against the spiritual forces of evil in
the heavenly realms (Eph. 6:12).

Before we can move out against these enemy forces, we must
submit to one another (see Eph. 5:21) and love one another,
including our spouses (see 5:25), fellow brethren (see 4:15,16)
and superiors (see 6:5-8). It is no accident that Paul laid out the
principles of unity and submission *before* introducing the principles of warfare and spiritual engagement (see Eph. 6:10-18).
This is because a house divided against itself cannot stand when
the attack of the enemy comes (see Mark 3:25).

When Paul taught the Ephesian Christians about spiritual
warfare, he said, "Finally, be strong" (Eph. 6:10). Tragically, there
are too many Christian casualties in the realm of spiritual warfare because misguided believers rush into chapter 6 and do not
live chapters 1 through 5.

The first five chapters reveal all that God has done for us and
given to us in Christ. Chapter 6 tells us that there is a devil and
that he commands wicked demonic forces who will do all they
can to oppose and hinder us from receiving what God desires to
give us and do through us. Like the Israelites in the book of
Joshua, the Promised Land is ours; but through warfare it still
must be possessed.

It was not long after our church began praying in this way
that all heaven broke loose in our church. People were getting
saved every week, and by God's grace we saw a transformation
take place among us. The church, which had been small for
decades, doubled, tripled and then quadrupled in size. Lives were
being radically changed by the power of God. We ministered to
dozens and dozens of people with healing and deliverance.

One Sunday evening the presence of God was so powerful that after the meeting, several of us ministered to people until 5:00 the following morning. That night God allowed me to understand in greater measure what He had spoken to me years before, revealing much about the city and the problems happening in our churches.

A traveling gypsy family had come that week to the church services and had responded to the call for salvation. From that moment on, all hell seemed to descend upon their family. That Sunday night as we ministered to the man's daughter, the father began to exhibit signs of a horrific demonic presence. This occurred even though the girl was in another room far away and he could not see what was taking place. As we prayed for the father, a terrifying, blood-curdling voice that was not his own spoke, boasting that the churches and ministers in our area had been cursed through blood sacrifices made on the hill nearby.

That night God brought great insight and victory. God was at work and His church was being healed and given insight into how to pray and evangelize. We now have in our church former prostitutes whose lives have been so changed by Jesus that they go out in teams to witness in the area. We have also opened a center for the homeless. We are seeing people from the vicinity come not only for shelter but also to find forgiveness and freedom from all kinds of addictions.

Thanks to the grace of God, we have not fallen prey to the sexual sins known to have beset the local churches of Aberdeen. Nevertheless, we have long struggled in the area of finances, trying to help people see that it is a blessing to honor God with their giving. Meanwhile, we battle to ensure that the financial atmosphere of our city does not find a place in our lives. It is heartbreaking to me when godly, generous people take offense because they fail to discern the spiritual powers of mammon at work in their own lives and their environment.

Now more than ever I recognize the schemes and strategies of the devil in the realm of money. Paul said to the church at Corinth, "We are not ignorant of his devices" (2 Cor. 2:11, *KJV*). Tragically, this has not always been the case. We as a local church have recently begun to know times of breakthrough in giving, but our greatest battles are still ahead . . . as are our greatest victories.

I share all this to help you realize that behind wealth and riches, evil powers can seek to gain control and rule over an individual, a city, even a nation. I want to share a few examples to accentuate this point.

Nazism and Communism are two ideologies that have arisen in this century, bringing with them death and misery on an unparalleled scale. Ideologically they could not be further apart, yet war and destruction have followed wherever they have gone.

## SPIRITUAL WARFARE AND NATIONS

In March 1998, I went to the Ukraine as part of a missions team from our church to deliver humanitarian aid and to support the churches with whom we were in contact. One of our Ukrainian interpreters, a young man named Roman, told us how much the people had suffered under Communism and the evil edicts of its leaders. According to this Ukrainian believer, in the 1930s more than 9 million Ukrainians died from forced famine carried out under the orders of Joseph Stalin, who wanted the nation to move to collective farming. To achieve this goal, Stalin ordered all food to be destroyed, creating mass starvation. Today in many towns and villages huge crosses—erected after the fall of Communism—stand as testimonies to this horrific event.

Roman told me about his own experiences with communist ideologies that were forced upon him as a child in school: "Children were made to sing about Lenin being in their heart. Even though he was dead, children were led to believe that his spirit lived on in them."

Communism is more than an ideology; it is a spirit from hell. In his book *Spiritual Warfare for Every Christian*, Dean Sherman tells the story of a missionary named Frank Barton (not his real name). In 1983, Barton began to make periodic visits to Romania as a nonresident missionary. Many he met were witness to the horrible acts of the secret police during Ceausescu's rule (1974–1989). All told, some 60,000 people died during the evil dictator's reign.[1]

Economic conditions were so severe that each home could run just one dim lightbulb for a few hours each night. So many babies froze to death in the hospitals that the government passed a law saying that a baby is not a person until it is one month old. This way their deaths did not show up on the statistics sheets.

As Barton traveled time after time to Romania, God led him to a small group of believers in a town called Timisora. This brave band met secretly in their homes, and God began to increase their awareness and understanding regarding spiritual warfare. They were told to pray against the spirits of fear and terror that were permeating every aspect of Romanian society. The Timisoran believers felt they were to go out in small groups late at night to prayer walk their town, praying against the principalities and powers in front of various official buildings.

They felt foolish, but they kept obeying God. Over a period of months things actually got worse. In February 1989, two pastors disappeared, murdered by the secret police; other believers were imprisoned. Still, the Christians continued to meet and pray, engaging in spiritual warfare. They refused to be intimidated. God was speaking to them, assuring them that victory was imminent.

Finally, on October 23, 1989, the members received a prophetic word, telling them that a fire would begin in their town and would blaze across Romania. The spark was indeed ignited in Timisora, just as God said. It began with the house arrest, on December 15, 1989, of a reformed pastor named Lazlo Tolkes. What usually followed such an arrest would be the disappearance of the minister, but this time things were different. Upon receiving word of Tolkes's house arrest, Christians streamed to the pastor's home, forming a human chain across the entrance. The police threatened them, but they began the first chant of a revolution that would see Communism crumble across eastern Europe and beyond: "Without fear! Without fear! Liberty!"

The number of Christians grew. Some were taken away and tortured while others were jailed. But instead of scattering, more came—thousands more. The believers walked up to soldiers and bared their chests to the gun barrels, declaring, "We are winning; down with Ceausescu."

The flame had been lit. The army turned around and fought the secret police alongside the people and Communism's brutal reign in their land was soon over.

Newspapers around the world reported the amazing events, claiming in headlines that fear and terror had been broken. Fear and terror—the same spirit powers God had directed a small group of Christian believers to pray against two years before—were now broken.[2]

## DEMONIC INFLUENCE AND NAZISM

What happened in World War II-era Germany was far more than another political movement calling for patriotic pride and fulfillment of national destiny. Nazism was founded on occultic philosophical beliefs and practices. Hitler and many of his closest aides were obsessed with astrology and ancient occultic beliefs, which contributed heavily to their beliefs in the supremacy of their race. Even the lightning strike and skull-and-crossbones insignia on S.S. uniforms were occultic signs used in witchcraft and satanic rituals. The same is true of the swastika. The Nazis' hatred of the Jews was more than an ideology; it was fueled by hell itself.

In William L. Shirer's authoritative book *The Rise and Fall of the Third Reich,* he records the works of Houston Stewart Chamberlain, whose writings and ideas fueled the beliefs and activities of Hitler and the Nazi party.

Chamberlain was one of the first intellectuals in Germany to see a great future for Hitler and Germany. He met Hitler in 1923 in Bayreuth and was so impressed that he wrote him the next day: "You have mighty things to do."

Shirer describes Chamberlain as

Hypersensitive and neurotic and subject to frequent nervous breakdowns. [He was] given to seeing demons who, by his own account, drove him relentlessly to seek new fields of study and get on with his prodigious writings. One vision after another forced him to change from biology to botany to the fine arts, to music, to philosophy, to biography, to history. Once in 1896, when he was returning from Italy, the presence of a demon became so forceful that he got off the train at Gardone, shut himself up in a hotel room for eight days and, abandoning some work on music that he had contemplated, wrote feverishly on a biological thesis until he had the germ of the theme that would dominate all his later works: race and history.[3]

Another of Chamberlain's books, *Foundations of the Nineteenth Century*, provided the Nazis with many of their racial aberrations. This book was a 1,200-page work that Chamberlain also wrote while "possessed" by his demons. In it, Chamberlain says that the key to history, indeed the basis of civilization, is race.[4]

We must look beyond the material realm to see the complete picture of what drives much of the evil in our society. From the death camps of Nazi Germany to the killing zones of Rwanda to the burned and pillaged villages of Kosovo, Satan has played a definitive role. Girding ourselves against the attacks of the enemy— whether in the areas of finances, personal morality or societal trends—is critical as we move forward in Christ (see Eph. 6:13-18).

**THE DEVIL DOES NOT REALLY MIND HOW MUCH WE OWN—AS LONG AS HE OWNS US.**

# SPIRITUAL WARFARE AND QUALITY OF LIFE

The devil does not really mind how much we have as long as he has us. Some of the poorest countries in the world are in bad shape because of demonic practice and idol worship—but so are some of the wealthiest nations. Through prosperity or poverty, it is the quality of our lives that the devil seeks to destroy and the destiny of our souls he desires to damn.

In recent years, Christians in the West have been amazed to hear reports of what God has been doing in China. As of this writing, there are more than 100 million followers of Jesus Christ in that vast Asian nation. Most of this growth has come during years of severe persecution. In his moving book *Secrets to Spiritual Success*, Paul Estabrooks relates personal stories of Chinese Christians, who have a great deal to teach us.

Estabrooks tells of one minister from Southern China, a Pastor Lamb, who says, "We have physical persecution but you have materialism. Your lot is harder because we know what we are fighting. Many times you don't."[5]

Another Chinese leader adds, "Once you are chasing after money there is no time and energy for church affairs. Our government knows that materialism will destroy the church faster than persecution can. I tell my co-workers in China that the biggest enemy we're facing is no longer communism; it is materialism."[6]

A Chinese believer who experienced much suffering for her faith expressed it this way:

We are constantly reminded that we are in spiritual warfare. We know for whom we are fighting. We know who the enemy is. And we fight. Perhaps we should pray for you Christians outside China. In your leisure, in your affluence, in your freedom, sometimes you can no longer realize that you are in spiritual warfare.[7]

Since coming to Aberdeen I have been aware of the strong materialistic powers at work in this city. At times I have to ask God to search my soul so that I do not become affected by the environment around me. Jesus said that if salt loses its saltiness it is no longer good for anything, except to be thrown out and trampled by men (see Matt. 5:13). But how can salt lose its salty properties? Only by the addition of impurities that corrupt and neutralize its flavor.

Usually this process of spiritual dilution takes place in tiny, seemingly insignificant increments. We begin to compromise and justify materialistic attitudes and actions, not realizing just how worldly we are slowly becoming. We soon get caught up in the world's system, its ways, its goals, its desires. Our daily prayer needs to be, "Search me, O God . . . see if there be any wicked way in me, and lead me in the way everlasting" (Ps. 139:23,24, *KJV*).

Ruth Graham tells the story of a Christian who had just arrived in a free country after years of persecution. He was appalled at the seeming casual commitment to Jesus and the materialistic contamination of the Christians. And he said so.

Some time later, he returned to visit the friend to whom he had spoken so bluntly when he first arrived. He asked if his friend remembered what he had said, the bitterness of his criticism. The friend remembered and tensed himself for a second attack. "I have come to apologize both for what I said and the way in which I said it," the immigrant said. "I was merely afraid. I did not know how dangerous freedom could be. It has been a year now and I am worse than those I criticized." Then he added a significant statement, "It is more difficult to live the Christian life under freedom than under repression."[8]

# GIVING AND SPIRITUAL WARFARE IN THE OLD TESTAMENT

In Isaiah 58, God spoke through the prophet Isaiah to rebuke the people of his day in what has come to be called the "fasting chapter." He criticized the Jews for thinking they could be spiritual in fasting while ignoring the spiritual laws of God and the social needs of others. In this passage we see that when we show love and compassion in giving to others, we break demonic powers:

> Is not this the kind of fasting I have chosen: to loose the chains of injustice and untie the cords of the yoke, to set the oppressed free and break every yoke? Is it not to share your food with the hungry and to provide the poor wanderer with shelter—when you see the naked, to clothe him, and not to turn away from your own flesh and blood?
>
> Then your light will break forth like the dawn, and your healing will quickly appear; then your righteousness will go before you, and the glory of the LORD will be your rear guard. Then you will call, and the LORD will answer; you will cry for help, and he will say: Here am I. If you do away with the yoke of oppression, with the pointing finger and malicious talk, and if you spend yourselves on behalf of the hungry and satisfy the needs of the oppressed, then your light will rise in the darkness, and your night will become like the noonday (Isa. 58:6-10).

William Booth and his wife, Catherine, lived and ministered in London more than a century ago. For the first 10 years of their marriage, William was in a quandary. *What is God calling me to do?* he wondered. One day when Catherine, a skillful Bible teacher, was invited to preach in London, God showed her husband what He was calling him to do.

William took a late-night walk through the slums of London's East End. Every fifth building was a pub. Most had steps at the counter, so little children could climb up and order gin. That night he told Catherine, "I seemed to hear a voice sounding in my ears, 'Where can you go and find such heathen as these and where is there so great a need for your labors?' Darling, I have found my destiny!"

Later that year in 1865, the couple opened the Christian Mission in London's slums. Their life vision was to reach the "down-and-outers" that other Christians had ignored. Together they founded the Salvation Army, a Christian organization whose evangelistic fervor for the lost was undergirded by a belief in the need for both social welfare and spiritual warfare. Booth later said, "Some men's ambition is art, some men's ambition is fame, some men's ambition is gold. My ambition is the souls of men."

The end of Booth's very last speech before his death in 1912 was filled with the passion and conviction that inspired countless others to work with him:

> While women weep, as they do now, I'll fight; while little children go hungry, I'll fight; while men go to prison, in and out, in and out, as they do now, I'll fight; while there is a drunkard left, while there is a poor lost girl upon the streets, where there remains one dark soul without the light of God, I'll fight! I'll fight to the very end.

Today the Salvation Army ministers through 3 million-plus members in 91 countries.

# REBUKING THE DEVOURER

The prophet Malachi told the people that when they honor God with their tithes and offerings, not only will the floodgates of heaven be opened, but also the devourer will be rebuked from their land (see Mal. 3:6-12). More pointedly, the Lord said to the people who cheated Him in their tithes and offerings:

You are under a curse—the whole nation of you—because you are robbing me (Mal. 3:9).

This does not mean that God loves His people any less when they fail to honor Him with their money. What happens is they remove themselves from under the blessing of His provision and protection. By withholding their tithes and offerings they make themselves vulnerable to enemy attack.

Let me ask you a question: Are you robbing God? Before you answer, read Malachi 3:6-12 and note that they robbed God not only with their tithes but also with their *offerings*. Do you tithe? What are your offerings like—i.e., what do you give above and beyond your tithe? Do you support the poor? Do you help other agencies or ministries? When anointed ministries come for special meetings to your church or area, do you give little when you are able to give more—while at the same time expecting much from God through their ministry? Or is your tithe all you ever give? Great battles are often won in spiritual warfare when God's people are liberated not only in their tithes but also in their offerings.

## GIVING AND SPIRITUAL WARFARE IN THE NEW TESTAMENT

In the parable of the unrighteous steward, Jesus taught that the way we handle worldly wealth determines how God will entrust us with true riches and spiritual things (see Luke 16:1-13). In the parable of the *minas* (a mina was about three month's wages),

Jesus said that those who use their wealth wisely will be allowed to rule over cities and exercise spiritual authority (see Luke 19:16-19).

In his book *Money, Sex and Power*, Richard Foster says, "As long as we think of money in impersonal terms alone, no moral problems exist aside from the proper use of it. But when we begin to take seriously the biblical perspective that money is animated and energized by 'powers,' then our relationship to money is filled with moral consequence."[9]

By "powers" Foster means fallen spiritual forces that Paul refers to in Ephesians 6:12 as "principalities and powers." Foster writes:

> Money is one of those fallen powers. When Jesus uses the Aramaic term mammon to refer to wealth (see Matt. 6:24), He is giving it a personal and spiritual character. He declares you cannot serve God and mammon. He is personifying mammon as a rival god and making it unmistakably clear that money is not some impersonal medium of exchange. . . . According to Jesus and all the writers of the New Testament, behind money are very real spiritual forces that energize it and give it a life of its own. Hence money is an active agent, it is a law unto itself and is capable of inspiring devotion. What we must recognize is the seductive power of mammon. Mammon asks for our allegiance in a way that sucks the human kindness out of our very being.[10]

I believe money can be used for good as well as evil. Nevertheless, we would do well to ponder and search our hearts with what Foster says. There are those who love not only what money can do but also what money *is*. They love to hold it and feel it. They are in love with its pursuit and possession, feeling privileged just to be able to accumulate and admire money.

Giving not only frees us from the tyranny of money but also confronts and conquers demonic powers that seek to keep us and our churches impoverished. So, why do Christians refuse to give or find it difficult to tithe?

Whether we realize it or not, we are battling against the world and its "me first" mentality. We are fighting the flesh, with its tenacity to pleasure itself. And we are warring against the devil, who wants to keep us bound by the pursuit of—and passion for—wealth. When we give freely, cheerfully and generously, we move in conquest over the world, the flesh and the devil.

*Notes*

1. Dean Sherman, *Spiritual Warfare for Every Christian* (Lynnwood, WA: YWAM Publishing, 1990), pp. 92, 93.
2. Ibid.
3. William L. Shirer, *The Rise and Fall of the Third Reich* (London: Mandarin Books, 1960), pp. 104-109.
4. Ibid.
5. Paul Estabrooks, *Secrets to Spiritual Success* (London: Sovereign World, 1996), p.166.
6. Ibid.
7. Ibid.
8. Ibid., p. 165.
9. Richard Foster, *Money, Sex and Power* (London: Hodder and Stoughton, 1985).
10. Ibid.

# CHAPTER 7

# GOD AND GAMBLING

*The worst thing that can happen to a man when he gambles is that he wins.*[1]

C. H. SPURGEON

Come with me for a moment to a hill and on it you will see three crosses. There hanging on the one in the center is Jesus, dying for the sins of the world. Below it you will notice a detachment of Roman soldiers, four of them, and their commanding officer. The four soldiers are not looking up to see what is taking place or listening to what is being said. They have their eyes down, waiting for the numbers to come up as they role a set of dice. They are gambling for the seamless robe Jesus had been wearing before He was stripped naked and beaten (see Mark 15:24). Only the commander looks up to see what is going on; the others are too busy to take notice.

Gambling can be a great distraction to the Cross.

Just before World War I a British politician and horse owner,

Mr. Horatio Bottomley, carefully devised "a sure way" of making a fortune. His plan was beautifully simple. Prior to a race at Blankengurghe in Belgium, he bought all six horses entered in the race. He then hired six English jockeys who were given careful instructions on what order to finish the race. Leaving nothing to chance, he backed all the horses as a precaution.

All was going well until halfway through the race when a thick sea mist rolled in and engulfed the racecourse. The jockeys could not see each other, and the judges could not see the horses. Only a few finished the race and in completely the wrong order. Mr. Bottomley ended up losing a fortune. Like many other gamblers before and since, he learned that a sure bet can be a very risky thing.[2]

# WHAT DOES THE BIBLE TEACH?

*Merriam Webster's Tenth Collegiate Dictionary* defines the verb "gamble" as "to play a game for money or property; to bet on an uncertain outcome." Gambling is the attempt to gain something for nothing at someone else's expense.

No one text in the Bible clearly defines what gambling is and whether it is right or wrong. It is one of those areas that some Christians believe to be acceptable and others believe to be totally wrong. Some Christians gamble but do so with a guilty conscience, justifying their actions with the caveat that gambling a dollar or two cannot be wrong. *Besides*, they think, *if I win I will give it to God's work.*

I once heard conference speaker and writer Edwin Louis Cole tell about a young lady in his church who asked him about dancing. The woman had said to him, "Pastor, you have taught us that we need to find a Scripture reference for everything to test whether a thing is right or wrong. Where does it say it's wrong to go disco dancing?"

He took her to Galatians 5:21 where it warns against the lust of the flesh, finishing with the phrase "and the like."

She said, "It doesn't mention disco dancing."

Cole replied, "Yes, it does." She asked where, and he answered, "And such like."

Ed Cole laughed as he told the story, but it does address the issue by asking, Is gambling of the flesh or of the spirit?

In reply to her son's questions, John Wesley's godly mother, Susanna, wrote this wise counsel to help him through his college days at Oxford:

> When you judge the lawfulness of a pleasure, take this rule: Whatever weakens your reason, impairs the tenderness of your conscience, obscures your sense of God or takes away the relish of spiritual things; whatever increases the authority of your body over your mind, that thing is sin for you however innocent it may be in itself.[3]

In the Old Testament, at times lots were cast by a priest to seek God's will in a given matter. A black stone and a white stone were used, black signifying no and white indicating yes. The belief behind casting lots in both the Old and New Testaments is summed up well in Proverbs 16:33: "The lot is cast into the lap, but its every decision is from the LORD." One form of casting lots was the sacred Urim and Thummim cast by the high priest (see Exod. 28:30). The scapegoat and the goat for sacrifice were chosen by lot (see Lev. 16:8-10); so were the tribal inheritances (see Num. 26:55,56).

The decision to go to battle was sometimes decided by lot (see Judg. 20:9). Lots were sometimes used to narrow the field down to a final choice, such as in the selection of Saul (see 1 Sam. 10:20-24) and the detecting of the cause for the defeat at Ai (see Josh. 7:16-18). Lots were also cast for the duties of priests (see Neh. 10:34; Luke 1:9), to determine who could live in Jerusalem (see Neh. 11:1) and for distribution of prisoners (see Joel 3:3). Matthias, the disciple chosen to replace Judas Iscariot, was chosen by lot (see Acts 1:26).

You may be asking whether or not casting lots is a form of gambling. No, it is not. We can toss a coin to remove any human decision; the biblical characters cast lots to specifically include God's decision. This was not luck, chance or fatalism—this was done by faith. After the Day of Pentecost we never hear of this method again, for a better way had come: The Holy Spirit was given to direct and lead God's people (see Acts 13:1,2).

# WHAT DOES JESUS SAY?

When Jesus was asked what was the greatest commandment, He said, "Love the Lord your God with all your heart and with all your soul and with all your mind" (Matt. 22:37). Gambling violates this statute because you cannot trust in God and in Lady Luck at the same time. In fact, the Bible makes it clear that God is to be our provider. Do we really believe He needs to do it through gambling? As Christians, we are to be stewards of all we have been given. Does God want us to use His resources in this way?

Jesus also identified the second greatest commandment: "Love your neighbor as yourself" (Matt. 22:39). Can we do this and seek to gain at our neighbor's expense? Does it benefit our society that a few seek to gain at the loss of others? Gambling destroys the distribution of wealth as it takes from the many and gives to the few. Gambling does not just take from the many; it takes from the poor, who can least afford it. The poor often sell their food stamps to play state-run lotteries. Why? They need hope, like everyone else. But their chances of actually winning are slim to the vanishing point. Gambling for them becomes just another tax on a limited income.

# CHURCH TRADITIONS

Generally, the Early Church fathers believed that gambling was wrong. Third-century Church father Tertullian said, "If you say you are a Christian while a dice thrower you are saying what you are not."

It is interesting to observe that during seasons of revival, not only have crime and drunkenness decreased, but gambling has as well. Christian researcher and author George Otis, Jr., in his book *Informed Intercession* (Ventura, CA: Renew Books, 1999), tells about the village of Almolonga in the highlands of Guatemala. Once ravaged by alcoholism and spousal abuse, now some 90 percent of the population have become Christian. Because of this local revival, all four jails in the city—once depositories for alcoholics and brawlers—have closed, and some have since become churches. If alcohol use and fighting decreased, it is probably safe to say that gambling fell as well.

William Wilberforce is a name usually associated with the abolition of the slave trade, but in 1826 he led the way for the abolition of the last state lottery in Great Britain. He saw clearly the power and effects of gambling in ruining and controlling so many lives.

Billy Graham writes:

The appeal of gambling is somewhat understandable. There is something alluring about getting something for nothing. I realize that, and that is where the sin lies. Gambling of any kind amounts to theft by permission. The coin is flipped, the dice is rolled or the horses run, and somebody rakes in that which belongs to another. The Bible says, "In the sweat of thy face shalt thou eat bread" (Gen. 3:19, *KJV*). It doesn't say, "By the flip of a coin shalt thou eat thy lunch." I realize that in most petty gambling no harm is intended, but the principle is the same as in big gambling. The only difference is the amount of money involved.[4]

## GAMBLING IN AMERICA TODAY

Why do people gamble? Why do Americans spend more than $25 billion on lottery tickets each year? Why do more than 90 million visit casinos annually?

No matter how you roll the dice, gambling is a bad proposition. In the January 1999 *Family News Letter* from Focus on the Family, James Dobson recounted the following facts:

[There is] a gambling fever that seems to have engulfed the nation and has penetrated every age group from the very young to the very old. Did you know that Americans gamble more money each year than they spend on groceries? Or that more than $600 billion is wagered legally in the United States annually? Or that five to eight percent of

American adolescents are already addicted to gambling? Or that 75 percent of pathological gamblers admitted that they had committed at least one felony to support their habit? Or that the massive Las Vegas casino called New York, New York was completed in 1996 at a cost of $460 million, and more than half of it was paid for in a period of one year only![5]

In this powerful and hard-hitting newsletter, Dobson reports some of the findings of The National Gambling Impact Study Commission that was set up by a bill passed in 1996. As one of those appointed to this commission, Dobson spent more that two years studying and analyzing the effects that gambling has on the nation. Some of the most tragic results were those experienced by families and children, and one of the more tragic stories he quotes illustrates this:

A 7-year-old girl was raped and strangled in a hotel casino, apparently by a young man who was captured on a surveillance videotape following her into a women's bathroom. Sherrice Iverson's body was discovered inside a locked corner stall in the bathroom at the Primadonna Casino in Primm, Nevada, about 40 miles from Las Vegas. The girl was slain early Sunday after security guards warned her father three times that night not to leave her alone in an arcade while he was gambling. The surveillance tapes show the girl possibly playing hide and seek in the arcade with two men in their late teens or early 20s.

At 3:48 A.M. the girl darted into the women's restroom, and one of the men followed her. The man came out alone 25 minutes later. After the girl's slaying, her father tried to cut a deal with the hotel, said a source, who spoke on condition of anonymity. "He said he wouldn't sue anybody if they would give him $100 to gamble with, free beer, fly his girlfriend in from out of town, and he wanted money for the arcade for the girl's 14-year-old brother."

One of the Las Vegas homicide detectives investigating Sherrice's killing said he was amazed by the number of unsupervised children at the Primadonna Hotel arcade. Based on a viewing of surveillance videos of the arcade, the officer said he counted at least 40 kids in the arcade at 3 in the morning, and didn't see any adults.[6]

# WHY DO PEOPLE GAMBLE?

People gamble for many reasons:

*Dissatisfaction.* Many never have enough and for them gambling is the only way to get rich quick. The greed factor becomes very destructive.

*Depression.* Gambling can provide a momentary thrill to alleviate depression, but this soon becomes a vicious cycle. As people gamble, they get high for a while, only to plunge into worse depression when they eventually lose.

*Despair.* Gambling is seen as a last hope. Nick Leeson, the man who broke the Barings Bank in England, found himself in this situation. The Japanese stock market went down as Leeson traded stocks and shares for his company. In sheer desperation, he continued to gamble greater amounts to try and gain back the losses. Eventually, he lost more than $1 billion and found himself in jail.

*Delight.* The temporary pleasure gambling brings is used by many to help relieve the boredom and monotony of life. They love the shouting and festive atmosphere of the racecourse, bingo hall or roulette table.

*Demonic compulsion.* There can be strongholds of demonic control that drive and compel people to gamble. The Bible tells of people controlled by demonic spirits, such as the demon-possessed man of the Gerasenes (see Mark 5:1-20) and the many demon-possessed people whom Jesus healed (see Matt. 8:16). Gamblers under demonic influence often lose their families' rent and food money to indulge the compulsion and fulfill the craving.

One pawnshop owner in Reno, Nevada, explained how casinos had impacted his business by displaying a jar of gold-filled human teeth that his customers had pulled and pawned.

Isaiah 65:11 warns against those "who spread a table for Fortune." In the Hebrew, this is a reference to the god Meni, whom some expositors think was an idol worshiped to bring luck and good fortune. Jesus spoke of the deceptive and destructive power of Mammon (see Matt. 6:24; Luke 16:13) who, as Richard Foster points out, is an animated

**WHEN WE OPEN OURSELVES UP TO THE LUST OF THE FLESH, WE ARE VULNERABLE TO THE DEVIL'S ONSLAUGHT.**

power. Mammon was also a god of money worshiped by the Chaldeans.

Powerful demonic forces are at work in the gambling meccas of America, where the average crime rate is 84 percent higher than in nongambling cities. The state of Nevada ranks first in America in suicide, divorce, high school dropouts and homicides against women. Nevada is at the top in gambling addictions, third in bankruptcy, third in abortion, fourth in rape, fourth in out-of-wedlock births, fourth in alcohol-related deaths, fifth in crime and sixth in the number of prisoners in its jails. It ranks in the top third of the nation in child abuse, and one-tenth of all southern Nevadans are alcoholics. One in 25 visitors who die in Las Vegas does so by taking his or her own life.[7]

I do not mean to say that every person who gambles is oppressed by demons, but when we open ourselves up to the lust of the flesh (i.e., greed and the pursuit of money), we are vulnerable to the devil's onslaught.

*Deception.* Jesus warned about the dangers and deceitfulness of wealth in the parable of the sower: "The seed that fell among the thorns is the man who hears the word, but the worries of this life and the deceitfulness of wealth choke it, making it unfruitful" (Matt. 13:22).

There are two great deceptions regarding gambling and wealth. The first is that money is the key to happiness—that it will make you free and independent. When you put your hope in money, a windfall may bring short-term happiness, but it is also sure to bring long-term heartache.

Take the case of a famous multibillionaire. All he ever really wanted in life was more. He wanted money, so he invested his inherited wealth into a billion-dollar pile of assets. He wanted more fame, so he broke into the Hollywood scene and became a film producer. He wanted more sensual pleasures, so he paid handsome sums to indulge his every sexual urge. He wanted more thrills, so he designed, built and piloted the fastest aircraft in the world.

This man was absolutely convinced that *more* would bring him true satisfaction. Unfortunately, history shows otherwise. By the end of his life, Howard Hughes was an emaciated, colorless, strung-out drug addict. He sported grotesque, inches-long fingernails that curled like corkscrews; his mouth was filled with black, rotting teeth. Hughes died believing the myth of *more*—a billionaire junkie, insane by all reasonable standards.[8]

The other deception regarding wealth centers on the "get rich quick" syndrome. People believe against all reasonable odds that they will be the next big winner. It is like gold fever.

Behavioral psychologist B. F. Skinner found he could teach a chicken to peck at a disk if he rewarded it with a piece of corn. If he stopped rewarding the chicken with corn, the chicken would stop pecking the disk. But if he gave an intermittent reward, that is, dropped a piece of corn only randomly, the chicken would peck at the disk until it was exhausted. This is the psychological principle behind the "get rich quick" syndrome. It is true that some people win huge jackpots—if there was not a winner now and again to feed the imagination, public obsession would soon die out. That is why the lottery sponsors go to great pains to publicize their big winners.

# A NEW MAN INSIDE

Many are familiar with the work and ministry of C. T. Studd. However, it was Studd's father, Edward, who brought the gospel into their home through the preaching of D. L. Moody. The elder Studd was enthralled with the preaching of Moody, whom

Studd would go hear preach night after night when the evangelist was in London. Studd became convicted of his sin and gave his life to Christ. But once he was a Christian, he found there were some aspects of his life of which he was uncertain. One of these was his gambling.

Studd had long been a great enthusiast of horse racing. He had an eye for fine horses; and he had successfully purchased, trained and raced horses, winning several steeplechases. He had achieved his greatest ambition when he won the English Grand National with a horse called Salamander.

D. L. Moody was preaching in London when Studd bought a horse superior to any he had ever owned. He immediately entered the horse in one of the major racing events, absolutely certain it would win. Full of excitement, he wrote to his good friend Mr. Vincent, saying, "If you are a wise man you will come to the race and put every penny you can on my horse." A few days later when he met up with his friend, Studd could not talk of anything but his new horse. He asked Vincent how much money he had wagered on the horse.

"Nothing," said Vincent.

"Then you are the biggest fool I ever saw," said Studd. "Nevertheless, come along and dine with me and you shall say where we are to go after dinner."

After dinner, Studd asked, "Now where shall we go to amuse ourselves?" Vincent suggested the Drury Lane Theatre. Studd strenuously objected, knowing that "those fellows," Moody and his colleague Sankey, were holding evangelistic meetings in the famed hall in London's theater district.

Despite feeling that Vincent had tricked him, Studd agreed to go along. The theater was crowded, but they managed to find seats just opposite the stage, almost under Moody's nose. Studd never took his eyes off Moody until he had finished his message.

Afterward Studd said to his friend, "I will come and hear this man again. He has just told me everything I have ever done." He kept his word and went again until he was soundly converted.

"In the afternoon of that day," wrote one of his sons later, "Father had been full of a thing that takes more possession of a man's heart and head than anything else, the passion for horse racing; and in the evening he was a changed man." Edward Studd's life had changed, but he wanted to be certain about whether or not he could continue with some of his former passions. His conscience had already told him he could not, so he decided to go and have it out with Moody.

Studd went to see Moody and said, "I want to be straight with you. Now that I am a Christian, shall I have to give up racing and shooting and hunting and theaters and balls?"

Moody replied, "Mr. Studd, you've been straight with me. I will be straight with you. Racing means betting and betting means gambling. I don't see how a gambler is going to be a Christian. Do the other things as long as you like."

Studd pressed the point. What did Moody really advise about the theater and cards? "Mr. Studd, you have children and people you love. You're now a saved man and you want to get them saved. God will give you some souls; as soon as ever you have won a soul, you won't care about any of the other things."

To the astonishment of his children and friends, Studd no longer pursued any of these passions, but seemed to care about only one thing: saving souls. He withdrew from horse racing and sold off his stable. He turned the great hall at his home in Tedworth into a preaching center and rode around the country inviting and urging the people to come. And they came by the hundreds. He wrote to his friends about their souls and laughed when they replied rudely. He called on his tailor and his shirtmaker and the man from whom he had bought his cigars, and spoke of Christ.

Studd lived just two more years after his conversion, but it was said at his funeral that he did more in two years than most Christians do in 20. A guest at Studd's house once remarked to the coachman that he "had heard that Mr. Studd had become religious or something."

"Well sir," said his coachman, "we don't know much about that, but all I can say is that though there's the same skin, there's a new man inside."[9]

*Notes*
1. Hannah Ward and Jennifer Wild, *The Lion Christian Quotation Collection* (London: Lion Publishing PLC, 1997), p. 191.
2. Stephen Pile, *The Book of Heroic Failures* (London: Futura Publications, 1979), pp. 111, 112.
3. Hannah Ward and Jennifer Wild, *The Lion Christian Quotation Collection*, p. 156.
4. Billy Graham, *The Billy Graham Christian Worker's Handbook* (Minneapolis, MN: World Wide Publications, 1984), p. 110.
5. James Dobson, *Family News Letter*, January 1999.
6. Ibid.
7. Ibid., as quoted from Sue Glick, The Violence Center, Washington, DC, September 1998.
8. Margaret Nicholas, *The World's Wealthiest Losers* (London: Chancellor Press, 1997), pp. 52, 53.
9. Norman Grubb, *C. T. Studd: Cricketer and Pioneer* (London: Lutterworth Press, 1970), pp. 11-15.

**CHAPTER 8**

# INVESTING IN GOD'S ECONOMY

*He who provides for this life and makes no provision for the life to come is wise for a moment but a fool forever.*[1]

JOHN TILLOTSON

*There are no pockets in a shroud.*

SPANISH PROVERB

I like the story of the theology student who was wrestling with a question he had about the fifth chapter of Revelation. He could not understand what was represented by the book that no one could open. He went to his minister for advice. "That's simple," said the minister. "It must be the checkbook."

You can take the blessing that God gives you—your treasures and talents—make a golden calf and fall down and worship it, or you can bring your gifts to God and let Him make a tabernacle where He dwells and reveals His glory. Money can either become an idol we serve or an instrument we use to worship God. It was the missionary E. Stanley Jones who said, "Whereas you cannot serve God and money, you can serve Him with it."

# WHAT ABOUT INSURANCE?

If you have ever filled out an insurance claim form, you know that the companies ask for the finest details of an accident. Often these companies receive the strangest replies. Here is a list taken from *First Choice* magazine published by Sun Alliance, a British insurance company:

- Coming home, I drove into the wrong house and collided with a tree I don't have.
- The guy was all over the road. I had to swerve a number of times before I hit him.
- The pedestrian had no idea which way to run so I ran him over.
- An invisible car came out of nowhere, struck my vehicle and vanished.
- A pedestrian hit me and went under my car.
- To avoid a collision I ran into a car.
- I knocked over a man but he admitted that it was his fault as he had been knocked over before.
- I was thrown from my car as it left the road. I was later found in a ditch by some cows.

Insurance is a premium we pay for protection against the loss of something we value or may be sued for. The insurance industry is huge and we are encouraged to insure everything. You name it and you can probably get some kind of insurance coverage for it. Professional baseball pitchers insure their pitching arms; world-class sprinters insure their legs—the list goes on. Some types of insurance are required by law while others are optional. Each person has to decide what is sensible and wise for themselves and their families. A lack of adequate coverage can be foolhardy, but excessive insurance for anything and everything can also be unwise stewardship of our resources.

It is not wrong to say you trust God and then buy a sensible insurance policy any more than it is to say God heals the sick and then take good care of your body to prevent illness.

Is there a difference between insurance and gambling? Insurance is not gambling when:

1. I do not insure to gain at the expense of another but only against the loss to myself or a related party. Examples would include auto insurance where coverage is required by law, or homeowner's insurance where the mortgage lender insists on insurance.
2. I am seeking to minimize the risks, not to increase them.
3. By not insuring I would be taking a gamble and could lose a great deal.
4. My motivation is not greed but good and wise stewardship of what God has given me.

## WHAT ABOUT INVESTMENTS?

I remember the night so clearly. The church was full. The atmosphere was electric. The guest speaker had been preaching about the second coming of Jesus, and I felt like it was going to happen that night! The preacher shared his frustration at having to pay toward a ministerial pension he would not be around to receive. That drew a loud laugh, but he had a point.

The meeting was so powerful that it had a profound effect on my young Christian life. I had just started working and had taken out an investment policy for the future. I decided after that night to cancel it, and I did. Today that policy would have been worth a great deal of money.

I later found out that the minister who spoke so passionately that night had to take early retirement years later, which made him grateful for his pension!

What then should we do about saving and investing for the future? Clearly, we should believe that God will provide for all our needs and that Jesus is indeed coming again soon. So why bother investing? No perfect, neat answer exists.

Some Christians do not bother to invest for the future and later regret it; others testify that God has looked after them well, even though they did not invest. God's guarantee of provision does not disqualify us from making wise investments, nor does Jesus' impending return excuse us from the requirement to exercise good stewardship. In His parable of the talents, Jesus encouraged wise stewardship of resources, which should be our guiding principle today (see Matt. 25:14-30). If it all belongs to God anyway, we certainly have a responsibility to steward what He has "loaned" to us.

Along the lines of stewardship, we should also consider the well-being of our loved ones if we are to pass on. That is why I believe it is a wise and loving act to create a will. Not only will you make it easier for those who must cope with their bereavement, but you are also taking steps to allocate what you want done with your estate. It gives joy to know that our holdings and belongings will bless others after we are gone.

Jesus did not condemn the practice of investing for the

future. In fact, the master in the parable of talents rewarded wise management of resources and punished fearful hoarding.

Many Christians have become wealthy by investing wisely and were then able to give generously to Christian work. One such man was William Colgate, the toothpaste and soap magnate, who became a member of a church in New York City. As a boy, he gave 10 cents of every dollar he made to the Lord's work. As his business prospered he gave 20 cents, his giving eventually rising to 50 cents of every dollar made. Once his children had finished their education, he gave *all* his income to God.[2] Other prominent industrialists who attributed their success to the fact that they were dedicated tithers include Heinz (ketchup), Kraft (cheese), Kellogg (cereal) and Crowell (Quaker Oats).

*Fortune* magazine recently reported that America's top 25 philanthropists gave away more than $1.5 billion in 1996. Of these 25, only four had inherited their fortunes. Most attributed their generosity in part to their religious backgrounds, and most were donors *before* they became wealthy.

Wise investments may include a home, pension (both private and state), savings accounts and insurance policies. But one of the greatest investments we can make is in our children. We can invest not only in their welfare and education but also by passing on a godly example of how to honor God with our lives and money. After all, our children are the only earthly things we will be able to take to heaven with us!

## WHEN DOES AN INVESTMENT BECOME A GAMBLE?

Some types of investment should be considered gambling while others would not. An investment is more likely to be a gamble when:

1. The transaction is short-term rather than long-term and I speculate for a quick buck.
2. It is based on guesswork and chance rather than knowledge.
3. I gain in such a way that there are bound to be losers.

**THE FUTURE IS IN GOD'S HANDS. WE MUST KEEP OUR EYES ON HIS DIVINE ECONOMY AND PLACE OUR TRUST IN THE LORD—NOT IN OUR INVESTMENTS.**

Let me share a word of warning because what may start as a wise investment can still become a snare engendering greed in your spirit.

My wife and I received some free shares of stock. We then purchased some more at a special price and saw them rapidly increase in value. This appeared to be a good investment. We were in it for the long term and with the free shares our investment was virtually risk free. Yet I soon found myself checking the shares every day to see how they were doing. After a while I knew the stock prices were feeding something in my flesh.

It is tragic when a Christian picks up the paper to see how his stocks are doing before he bothers to pick up his Bible. I did not want to ever come to that place, so I sold the shares and got out of the stock market. I had begun to feel the shares owned me more than I owned the shares.

Again, the Bible does not condemn the practice of planning for the future. Jesus did not say take no thought for tomorrow in the sense of not preparing for it. What He did say was do not worry about it (see Matt. 6:25). He sent out His disciples without a purse or money (see Luke 10:4), but once they had learned to depend fully on God for their provision, He later sent them out and told them to take a purse (see Luke 22:36).

The future is in God's hands, as are all our investments. If economies collapse and banks and companies are ruined, our portfolios and pensions could be wiped out. That is why we must keep our eyes on God's divine economy and place our trust in Him—not in our investments.

# WHAT ABOUT SAVINGS?

Do you ever feel a little uneasy when you have some money put away and then hear about a need for missions or receive letters making appeals for God's work? How do you respond? I trust it is with generosity. But we need to recognize that we cannot meet every need and God does not ask us to. He wants us to respond to those needs to which He calls us. When we experience that surge of joy and rise in faith and compassion, it is a good indication that the Holy Spirit is prompting us to send financial aid.

Savings are not wrong unless you are obsessed with them. There is a big difference between storing and hoarding. When you hoard something, it becomes your security, something not to be shared. Storing is different; it is positioning yourself so that you are able to respond to a need when the Holy Spirit speaks to you about it. So ask yourself this question, *Are my savings something I hoard for myself or something I store as a steward of what God has given me?*

# WHAT ABOUT RETIREMENT?

The thriving postwar economy of the late '40s and the 1950s gave retiring Americans of that generation the benefits of improved Social Security and increasingly better pensions. However, the future of the Social Security system is not so bright. Between 1946 and 1964, 76 million baby boom children were born. This mass of people will have a huge effect on the benefits system and on retirement figures in the near future.

By the year 2030, 20 percent of the population will be over 65, compared to 12.6 percent in 1990. In the next 20 to 30 years, average life expectancy in the U.S. is conservatively projected to be 83 years for women and 77 years for men.

What does all this mean? It means there are some big changes ahead. The work force is shrinking in comparison to the number of people receiving state pensions. This will place an overwhelming burden on the benefits system. People will likely not be able to rely upon the state for their future income and security. Wise investment and planning now will save a great deal of despair and dependency in the years to come.

# LIVING BY FAITH

All Christians are called to live by faith, but what does that mean? You can live by faith like George Mueller, the Englishman who saw more than 25,000 answers to prayer and who saw God provide every penny to run his orphanages without advertising the need or appealing for money. You can live by faith like Francis of Assisi, who went around asking for money and for people to support him. You can live by faith by working and earning a regular income; the Bible makes it clear that God has called us to work for our income when we are able to do so. You can live by faith while living off your investments. We live by faith when we are living the way God tells us to live.

George Mueller's faith statement was, "No more going to man instead of going to God." In his 70 years of ministry, the equivalent of more than $70 million passed through his hands for his orphanages. He fed, clothed and educated as many as 2,000 orphans at a time, without ever asking for a penny or even making his own needs known.

Another $35 million was spent by his Scriptural Knowledge Institute for the international distribution of Bibles, tracts and educational materials. In his lifetime he gave away the equivalent of more than $18 million to missions through his ministry—all out of the overflow of God's abundant supply.

The following is an extract from Mueller's diary on August 18, 1838: "I have not one penny in hand for the orphans. In a day or two again many pounds will be needed. My eyes are upon the Lord."

That evening, he wrote:

Before this day is over, I have received from a sister £5. She had some time since put away her trinkets, to be sold for the benefit of the orphans. This morning, whilst in prayer, it came to her mind, *I have this £5, and owe no man anything, therefore it would be better to give this money at once, as it may be some time before I can dispose of the trinkets.* She therefore brought it, little knowing that there was not a penny in hand and that I had been able to advance only four pounds, fifteen shillings and five pence for housekeeping in the boys' orphan house, instead of the usual ten pounds.

On August 23, Mueller wrote, "Today I was again without one single penny when £3 was sent from Clapham, with a box of new clothes for the orphans."

Mueller was later to look back on the period from 1838 to 1846 as the time of the greatest trials in his work with the orphans. These were not years of continuous difficulty; rather, there tended to be a pattern of a few months of trial, followed by some months of comparative plenty. During the whole period, according to Mueller, the children knew nothing of his trials.

In the midst of one of the darkest periods, he recorded, "These dear little ones know nothing about it, because their tables are as well supplied as when there was £800 in the bank, and they have lack of nothing."

At another time he wrote, "The orphans have never lacked anything. Had I thousands of pounds in hand, they would have fared no better than they have, for they have always had good, nourishing food, the necessary articles of clothing, etc." In other words, God supplied their need day by day, even by the hour. Enough was provided, but no more than enough.

## SILVER AND GOLD HAVE I NONE

Now a man crippled from birth was being carried to the temple gate called Beautiful, where he was put every day to beg from those going into the temple courts. When he saw Peter and John about to enter, he asked them for money. Peter looked straight at him, as did John. Then Peter said, "Look at us!" So the man gave them his attention, expecting to get something from them. Then Peter said, "Silver or gold I do not have, but what I have I give you. In the name of Jesus Christ of Nazareth, walk." Taking him by the right hand, he helped him up, and instantly the man's feet and ankles became strong. He jumped to his feet and began to walk (Acts 3:2-8).

Tradition has it that Pope Innocent IV and Thomas Aquinas were standing together watching bags of gold being carried into the Vatican. "You see," said Pope Innocent, "the day is past when the Church has to say, 'Silver and gold have I none.'"

"Yes," Thomas is said to have responded, "and neither can she say to the lame man, 'In the name of Jesus, rise up and walk.'"

When the apostle Peter spoke these words in Jesus' name, he said them to a middle-aged man born crippled who was begging for money at the entrance to the Temple. Peter had no money. After all, the apostles' treasurer, Judas, had run off with it all before committing suicide. What Peter *did* have may not have been what the man wanted, but it was what he needed.

When we invest in God's economy, the results are sometimes miraculous. During the 1940s a woman named Chen was an effective itinerant evangelist in China. Her husband, a teacher, was interned in a labor camp; and her oldest son, Peter, a young teenager, was martyred by the Red Guards during the infamous Cultural Revolution.

Chen was left alone to care for her three remaining children, all under 10 years of age. Yet God commanded her to continue her evangelistic preaching tours. So, she continued to put herself at risk because she loved God above all else. Here is how she described one incident of God's provision for her family.

One day I said to my children, "The Lord has told me that today I will go to prison for him. Father is not at home so please behave. Love each other and don't forget to bring food for your mom." During that time there were so many prisoners that the government could not provide food for all of them, so family members provided food.

The children cried when they heard this. Daniel, one of the sons, retorted, "But mom, we have only five catties of rice left. How can we have rice and also send you some? When it's all gone we'll die."

I told the children, "The Lord can turn nothing into something." I reminded them of the story of Elijah and the widow. They had simple childlike faith and believed that God would provide for their needs. So they concluded, "Even though our rice is not enough, we will cook for you too."

After talking with the children, the Public Security Bureau personnel came to the door and arrested me. Daniel followed me to the prison to find out which cell I would be in. The younger two children knelt in prayer. As I was taken away my heart was wrenched as I heard their little voices trailing off.

I was in prison on that occasion for 30 days. All the while Daniel faithfully sent rice for me. When I returned home I asked, "Is there any rice left?" Daniel's response was, "Mom, our rice container is overflowing." It really was. Those five catties of rice had inexplicably grown to about 40 catties and were literally overflowing the container. I said, "Praise the Lord! Now we can cook for other inmates and feed them as well." The Lord's grace is beyond measure.[3]

# WHAT ABOUT TREASURES ON EARTH?

Jesus constantly warned his followers about the dangers of money. Wealth is deceptive and destructive because it attaches us to the world. By "the world" I do not mean the universe, the environment or a collection of people and nations (a benign use of the word), but rather an outlook and mind-set that affects the way we see the whole of life. The world is a complex of intellectual, emotional and spiritual systems that orient themselves against God and His purposes.

All our temptations have to do with the world. The devil is the tempter, we are the tempted, and the world is the temptation. Jesus taught in the Sermon on the Mount that the attack of the world comes in two main forms. First, there may be a seemingly positive love of the world. Second, there may be anxiety and fear regarding it. Jesus warned:

Do not store up for yourselves treasures on earth, where moth and rust destroy, and where thieves break in and steal. But store up for yourselves treasures in heaven, where moth and rust do not destroy, and where thieves do not break in and steal. For where your treasure is, there your heart will be also (Matt. 6:19-21).

By "treasures on earth," Jesus was talking about much more than money. Earthly treasure includes fame, position, power and status—everything that attaches us to this world's values and ideals. Jesus was not saying these things are wrong in and of themselves, but our attitude and relationship with them can make us worldly.

# WHAT IS THE BEST INVESTMENT?

Voltaire was a famous writer and reformer and the most influential figure of the French Enlightenment. "Crush the infamous" was the famous slogan he raised against the Church, Christianity and intolerance. He constantly vilified the Jews, especially the ancient Hebrews, as superstitious fanatics guilty of producing the Bible, Jesus Christ and, hence, Christianity.

The nurse who was present at Voltaire's deathbed was later asked to attend to an Englishman who was critically ill. She asked, "Is he a Christian?"

"Yes," came the reply, "but why do you ask?"

"Sir," she answered, "I was the nurse who attended Voltaire in his last illness, and for all the wealth of Europe I would never see another infidel die."

It is reported that Voltaire cried out with his dying breath, "I am abandoned by God and man! I shall go to hell."[4]

On his deathbed, enlightened thinker and author Thomas Paine is purported to have said, "I would give worlds if I had them if *The Age of Reason* had never been published. Stay with me; it is hell to be left alone."[5]

Atheist and political philosopher Thomas Hobbes, in his last moments, said, "I am taking a fearful leap into the dark."[6]

What are you doing with your life? What are you investing in? What will you be remembered for? In 1867, the Swedish chemist Alfred Nobel invented a new high explosive that he named "dynamite." He was convinced that his invention had made war too horrible to ever happen again, but he quickly discovered there was no shortage of buyers for his new explosive. Nobel made a huge fortune from its sales, yet was horrified with the suffering and misery it caused in wars and conflicts. But what was he to do?

Toward the end of the nineteenth century, he awoke one morning to read his own obituary in the local paper: "Alfred Nobel, the inventor of dynamite, who died yesterday, devised a way for more people to be killed in a war than ever before, and he died a very rich man."

Actually, it was Alfred's older brother who had died; a newspaper reporter had confused the epitaph. But the account had a profound effect on Alfred. He decided he wanted to be known for something other than developing a means for killing people efficiently and for amassing a fortune in the process. The result was the initiation of the Nobel Prize, the prestigious award for scientists and writers who foster peace. Nobel said, "Every man ought to have the chance to correct his epitaph in midstream and write a new one."[7]

Two men were talking one day about a mutual friend who had just died. "I wonder just how much he left?" asked one.

"I can tell you exactly," said the other. "Everything."

When Alexander the Great died, he gave instructions that his body be positioned in his coffin so that people could see his open, empty hands. He was well aware that he could not take any of his conquests with him.

Michael Chang, the great tennis player, commenting on his career and his faith said, "The money's great, but it won't last. The honor's great, but it won't last. What will last is the love of Christ in my heart."

Among D. L. Moody's last words were, "This is glorious! Earth is receding, heaven is opening, God is calling me." For the man of God, death was not a fearful leap. This, he said, was his homecoming, falling into the arms of Jesus.

When we die, we leave behind all that we have and take with us all that we are. Invest wisely in the area that pays eternal dividends. That is how to succeed in God's economy.

*Notes*

1. Hannah Ward and Jennifer Wild, *The Lion Christian Quotation Collection* (London: Lion Publishing PLC, 1997), p. 136.
2. Tom Rees, *Money Talks* (London: Billing and Sons Ltd., 1963), p. 47.
3. Paul Estabrooks, *Secrets to Spiritual Success* (London: Sovereign World, 1996), pp. 20, 21.
4. Walter B. Knight, comp., *Knight's Master Book of New Illustrations* (Grand Rapids, MI: Eerdmans Publishing Co., 1956), p. 159.
5. A. Naismith, *1200 More Notes, Quotes and Anecdotes* (London: Pickering and Inglis Ltd., 1975), p. 68.
6. Ibid.
7. Doug Murren and Barb Sharin, *Is It Real When It Doesn't Work?* (Nashville, TN: Thomas Nelson, 1990).

# CHAPTER 9

# GAINING THE WORLD AND LOSING YOUR SOUL

*When the Holy Spirit enters the heart of man, He shows him all
his inner poverty and weakness, the corruption of his soul and heart,
and his remoteness from God.*

INNOCENT VENIAMINOV

*The real measure of our wealth is how much we'd be worth
if we lost all our money.*

JOHN HENRY JOWETT

A man of great wealth was asked to contribute to a major financial campaign within a church. The urgent need and compelling
case were stated and he was asked for his support. He responded, "I understand why you think I can give $50,000. I am a man

with my own business and it is true, I show all the signs of affluence. But there are some things you don't know. Did you know
that my mother is in an expensive nursing home? Did you know
that my brother died with a family of five and left them in great
need? Don't you realize that I have a son who is deeply religious,
has gone into social work and is making less than the national
poverty level to meet the needs of his family?"

"No, we hadn't realized," they replied.

"Well then, if I don't give any of them a cent, why do you
think I'll give it to you?"

Then there was the occasion when the huge brass collection
plates were passed around the English congregation one Sunday
evening and returned almost empty to the vicar. He took them,
held them up to heaven and prayed, "Lord, we thank You for the
safe return of these plates."

When it comes to giving, some people stop at nothing. Some
give out of their means while others give out of their meanness.
On the subject of meanness, I was intrigued by an article in a
January 1994 edition of the *British Daily Express*, which began,
"Architect Tyle Steen is the meanest man on earth and he can
prove it. For the 33-year-old from Sydney, Australia, has won the
world's greatest skinflint contest." How did he achieve this? The
article went on to list his catalog of stinginess. His wife, Angela,
had astonished the judges by telling them how he:

- charged his two sons £1 a day for helping with their
  homework;
- made visiting relatives pay for their food;
- had his hair cut at the local dog parlor because it was
  cheaper; and
- bought a pay toilet from the local bus station, so he
  could charge visitors for using his toilet.

Married to the man for 13 years, Mrs. Steen added, "I knew he was a money grabber as soon as we wed; he canceled our honeymoon because it was too expensive."

# THE RICH FOOL

The ancient Aztecs of Mexico used their captives as human sacrifices to their gods. Before offering up their prisoners, however, they sometimes allowed them to live in luxury and ceremonial splendor for a whole year—but then came pay day.

Jesus frequently warned about the destructiveness and deceitfulness of wealth. In Luke 12:13-21, Jesus told a story about a man who only lived for himself and was controlled by the accumulation of wealth. Jesus told this parable in response to a man who came and requested that Jesus speak to the man's brother about the division of their family estate.

Jewish law was quite definite on this point: The eldest son received two-thirds of the estate, while one-third was given to the younger son or divided among the younger sons. Covetousness had taken hold in the sharing of this inheritance, however, and Jesus was being asked to intervene. Whether the elder brother was wanting more than his share or the rest of the family was after more is uncertain. The saying "Where there's a will there's a relative" was as true then as it is now.

In response, Jesus bypassed the specifics of the case and went to the root of the problem with this warning about greed:

> The ground of a certain rich man produced a good crop.
> He thought to himself, "What shall I do? I have no place
> to store my crops." Then he said, "This is what I'll do. I
> will tear down my barns and build bigger ones, and there

I will store all my grain and my goods. And I'll say to myself, 'You have plenty of good things laid up for many years. Take life easy; eat, drink and be merry.'" But God said to him, "You fool! This very night your soul will be demanded from you. Then who will get what you have prepared for yourself?" This is how it will be with anyone who stores up things for himself but is not rich toward God (Luke 12:16-21).

The rich fool was destined to become the richest man in the cemetery. Society's remembrance of him would have spoken of success and achievement. Had he lived, he might have won awards for his industry and enterprise. Invitations for speaking engagements would have poured in from businesses and conventions. But God sees behind the achievement and beyond the earthly accolades, and His verdict is, "You fool."

In 1923, at the Edgewater Beach Hotel in Chicago, Illinois, seven of the most powerful money magnates in the world gathered for a meeting. Their combined wealth and assets controlled more money than the U.S. Treasury. In that group were Charles Schwab; Richard Whitney, president of the New York stock exchange; Arthur Cotton, a wheat speculator; Albert Fall, a presidential candidate and a very wealthy man; Jesse Livermore, one of the richest men on Wall Street; Leon Fraser, president of the International Bank of Settlements; and Ivan Kruger, who headed the largest monopoly in America. But what happened to them?

Charles Schwab died penniless. Richard Whitney spent the rest of his life serving a jail sentence in Sing Sing prison. Arthur Cotton went bankrupt. Albert Fall was pardoned from a federal prison, so he might die at home. Leon Fraser, Jesse Livermore and Ivan Kruger all committed suicide.[1]

In another confrontation with the wealthy, Jesus spoke plainly with a rich young ruler who came to Him to ask how he could have eternal life. The privileged young man received a startling reply: "Go, sell your possessions and give to the poor, and you will have treasure in heaven. Then come, follow me" (Matt. 19:21). Upon hearing this, the wealthy young man walked away, despondent.

> Then Jesus said to his disciples, "I tell you the truth, it is hard for a rich man to enter the kingdom of heaven. Again I tell you, it is easier for a camel to go through the eye of a needle than for a rich man to enter the kingdom of God."
>
> When the disciples heard this, they were greatly astonished and asked, "Who then can be saved?"
>
> Jesus looked at them and said, "With man this is impossible, but with God all things are possible" (Matt. 19:23-26).

The disciples' amazement was due primarily to their distorted belief that the wealth of the rich young ruler was a sign of God's special favor upon him. But Jesus went to the heart of this young man's problem: The man had failed to realize that he did not possess his riches, but they possessed him.

# TREASURE IN HEAVEN?

As you read the following stories ask yourself which of these individuals were truly prosperous.

## BARBARA HUTTON

You may never have heard of Barbara Hutton, but you will almost certainly know about Woolworth's, the department store chain. As heiress to the Woolworth fortune, Hutton was worth millions and had everything money could buy. Her last public appearance revealed an emaciated, frail woman dripping with jewels, her eyes hidden behind enormous sunglasses.

Years earlier, in 1930, her father Frank Hutton gave Barbara a coming-out party. A thousand socialites were invited and the cost was estimated at well over $60,000, this at a time when most people were reeling from the Wall Street crash.

Her first marriage set the pattern for the six to come. Desperate for love and happiness, she married Prince Alexis Mdivani, whom she found devastatingly attractive. On their wedding night he told her she was too fat, and he behaved very coldly toward her. For years after, she waged a constant battle against her weight, causing her great distress and unhappiness.

When she was 21, she took full, unrestricted control of her immense fortune. It was estimated that if she spent $10,000 dollars a day for 10 years, she still would have made only a small dent in her bank account. But this failed to bring her what she longed for most: lasting love and happiness.

When she married her third husband, movie star Cary Grant, it was obvious they were both very much in love. They had everything, but for her it was not enough. Something else was driving her and soon her old restless nature resurfaced; endless parties and spending sprees followed. Grant could not understand or cope with it all and three years and seven weeks after they married, they divorced.

To console herself she bought a palace in Tangier and married again, this time to another handsome prince. She told the press, "I have never been happier. We will be on our honeymoon for 30 or 40 more years." Two years later she was divorced again. By this time she was suffering terribly from insomnia and the physical toll from years of semistarvation.

Near the end of her life, despite her massive wealth, she was just a vulnerable, sick 66-year-old woman riddled by loneliness. "I inherited everything but love," she told her friend and biographer Philip Van Rensselaer. "I've always been searching for it, because I didn't know what it was." She married seven times, searching for the man who would fulfill her dreams. At her bedside when she died there were some friends, but no husband.[2]

## ARISTOTLE ONASSIS

They called him "The Golden Greek," a billionaire who owned an island like a demiparadise, a yacht like a floating palace, half of Monaco, an airline, one of the world's largest shipping fleets and beautiful houses.

Aristotle Onassis was 46 when he first married. His bride was Athina Livanos, whom he first met when she was just 14. He waited three years to make her his wife. They had two children during their 13 years of marriage, Alexander and Christina.

Athina filed for divorce in 1959 after Onassis had a two-year affair with opera singer Maria Callas. Part of Athina's divorce statement was significantly revealing: "It is almost 13 years since Mr. Onassis and I were married in New York City. Since then he has become one of the world's richest men, but his great wealth has not brought me happiness with him, nor, as the world knows, has it brought him happiness with me."

Onassis's relationship with Callas also ended in tears. She grew so distraught that she did not want to sing anymore; she canceled concerts at the last moment and went for months without practicing a note. Onassis began to treat her so badly that her friends begged her to leave him before he broke her heart.

At this stage in his life, Onassis believed that, materially, he had achieved everything he wanted and began moving in very high social and political circles. When he heard that Jacqueline Kennedy was suffering deep depression after the death of her baby son, Patrick, he gave her full use of his yacht. He stocked it with caviar, the finest vintage wines and exotic fruits and took the First Lady on a cruise. When he learned about John F. Kennedy's assassination, he flew from Hamburg to Washington and was one of the few nonfamily mourners at the White House.

For the next few years he and Jackie spent a lot of time together, and they married in October 1968. Alexander and Christina were shattered by the news. Alexander remarked scathingly, "It's a perfect match. My father loves names, and Jackie loves money." Onassis found that marrying a woman as famous as Jackie had its drawbacks. He was intensely proud and found it hard to be continually upstaged by his wife wherever they went.

Jackie loved to spend. Often, her answer to a problem was to indulge in her love of clothes. In the first year of her marriage she went on a shopping spree, spending more than $1.25 million in the fashion houses of the world.

On the evening of Sunday, July 21, Onassis's aircraft crashed on takeoff from Athens. Alexander was dragged alive from the wreckage but died the following day. Onassis's grief was so great that, at first, he would not part with his son's body for burial. But the worst part of his grief was guilt. His son had warned him that the Paiggio airplane used by his father's airline was a death trap.

Onassis was inconsolable. He could not sleep and walked the deck of his luxury yacht alone at night. Back on his island paradise of Skorpios, he roamed the island until dawn and spent hours sitting beside his son's tomb.

His marriage with Jackie continued to deteriorate, and Onassis became seriously ill. His condition was diagnosed by specialists as myasthenia gravis, a disease that turns the body against itself. In his case, the ailment was brought on by stress, fatigue and too much alcohol. He had become so alienated from Jackie that he had cut her out of his will, leaving almost everything to his daughter, Christina. He died in Paris, exhausted and under sedation, with Christina at his bedside and Jackie detained in New York.

The Onassis fortune did not bring happiness for Christina, either. Just 13 years later, at age 38, she was found dead in Buenos Aires at the house of a friend. She was in the throes of divorce from her fourth husband and fighting a losing battle with her weight.[3]

## DAVID LIVINGSTONE

When H. M. Stanley found missionary David Livingstone in Central Africa, he asked Livingstone to return to England with him. Livingstone refused to go, but he sent letters to his family. Two days later he wrote in his diary: "March 19th, my birthday. My Jesus, my King, my life, my all. I again dedicate my whole self to thee. Accept me and grant, O gracious Father, that ere the year is gone I may finish my work. In Jesus' name I ask it. Amen."

A year later Livingstone's servant entered his hut late in the night and found the old man kneeling beside his bed, his head buried in his hands upon the pillow. He was evidently praying when he died. His friends carried his embalmed body for 11 months across Africa to transport him via sailing ship to England, where he is buried in Westminster Abbey in London. Livingstone's heart, however, is buried in Africa.

His brother, John Livingstone, is buried in Ontario, Canada. John died one of the richest men in the province. The two boys grew up together in a simple Scottish home under the same instruction and example. John lived in luxury and died in wealth. Yet when he died, there was a brief note in the newspapers stating that he was the brother of David Livingstone, "the well-known missionary in Africa."

David Livingstone's fortitude and confidence could be seen when he spoke at Glasgow University in 1896, after having been awarded a Doctorate of Law. He rose to speak and was received in respectful silence. He was gaunt and haggard as a result of hardships in Africa. His left arm, crushed by a lion, hung helplessly at his side as he announced his resolve to return to Africa, without misgiving and with great gladness.

He added, "Would you like me to tell you what supported me through all the years of exile among a people whose language I could not understand, and whose attitude toward me was often uncertain and often hostile? It was this, 'Lo, I am with you always, even unto the end of the age.' On these words I staked everything, and they never failed."[4]

**"'LO, I AM WITH YOU ALWAYS, EVEN UNTO THE END OF THE AGE.' ON THESE WORDS I STAKED EVERYTHING, AND THEY NEVER FAILED."**

**DAVID LIVINGSTONE**

## C. T. STUDD

I have already told the story of the wealthy Edward Studd, who was converted through D. L. Moody's ministry. His son, C. T. Studd, was given everything a boy could wish for. He possessed fame, fortune and talent and was a national hero as captain of England's cricket team. But he gave it all away to find something even greater—he went to serve Christ in China and Africa. He said, "Some want to live within the sound of a church or chapel bell. I want to run a rescue shop within a yard of hell."

It was an article by an atheist that spurred him to all-out dedication for Christ. The atheist's words read:

If I firmly believed, as millions say they do, that knowledge and practice of religion in this life influences destiny in another, then religion would mean to me everything. I would cast away earthly enjoyments as dross, earthly cares as follies, and earthly thoughts and feelings as vanity. Religion would be my first waking thought, and my last image before sleep sank me into unconsciousness. I should labor for its cause alone. I would take thought for the morrow of eternity alone. I would esteem one soul gained for heaven a life worth suffering.

Earthly consequences would never stay my hand or seal my lips. Earth, its joys and griefs, would occupy no moment of my thoughts. I would strive to look upon eternity alone, and on the immortal souls around me, soon to be everlastingly happy or everlastingly miserable. I would go forth to the world and preach to it in season and out of season, and my text would be, "What shall it profit a man if he gain the whole world and lose his own soul?"[5]

Studd married a Salvation Army girl, Cilla, and together they served God. When he first went to China, God spoke to him through the story of the rich young ruler who was told to sell his possessions, give to the poor and follow Christ. He knew this was God's calling for him and with determined—but not hasty or foolish—decision, he set about doing just that, knowing that God had promised to meet all his needs.

He sat down and wrote out several checks. One was to George Mueller for the work of the orphanages he ran in Bristol; another was for Booth Tucker for the Salvation Army's work in India. Then he sent a large sum to D. L. Moody, hoping that Moody would establish a mission work in India, because it was there that Studd's father had made most of his fortune. Moody said he had no plans to establish such a work in India, but he would do the next best thing: open a Bible college to train young people for the ministry and mission field. Thus the Moody Bible Institute was born.

Studd kept back a small sum for his own provision; now that he was married he felt the responsibility to provide adequately for his wife. But Cilla was not to be outdone. She said, "C. T., what did Jesus tell the rich young ruler to do?"

C. T. replied, "Sell all and give to the poor."

She said, "Then give it all, for it is safer to invest in the bank of heaven than in the Bank of England, which is quite likely to break on Judgment Day."

C. T. Studd wrote his last check to William Booth, who had been praying for finances to send workers overseas. He said, "I have never been in want in China, Africa, London or elsewhere and if Christ be God and gave all for me, how can any sacrifice I make be too great for Him?"[6]

# WHAT ARE OUR PRIORITIES?

Our life is the sum total of thousands of decisions we make along the way. Press toward the goals that Paul gave us in Philippians 4:8: "Whatever is true, whatever is noble, whatever is right [e.g., proper priorities with money and wealth], whatever is pure, whatever is lovely, whatever is admirable—if anything is excellent or praiseworthy—think about such things."

There is a story that comes from the 1912 sinking of the Titanic of a frightened woman who, having found a place in a lifeboat, suddenly thought of something she needed. She asked permission to return to her stateroom before they cast off. She was granted three minutes or they would leave without her.

She rushed across the deck that was already listing at a dangerous angle. She raced through the gambling room, thousands of dollars sloshing about her ankles as she slogged through the water. She came to her stateroom and pushed aside her diamond rings and jewelry as she reached for a shelf above her bed and grabbed three small oranges. She quickly found her way back to the lifeboat and climbed back in.

This may seem incredible as just 30 minutes before, a thousand crates of oranges would have seemed worthless in comparison to a single diamond. But death had boarded the Titanic. Instantaneously, values had been altered and priorities changed.

When the city of Pompeii was being excavated, a body was found embalmed by the ashes of Vesuvius from the eruption of A.D. 79. The woman's feet were turned toward the city gate, but her face was turned backward toward something that lay just beyond her outstretched hands. The prize for which those frozen fingers were reaching was a bag of pearls. Death was hard at her heels and life was beckoning beyond the city gates, but she could not shake off the spell of wealth.

When your epitaph is written—on the hearts of your family or perhaps in the morning paper—what will it say? It is true that the higher we climb on the world's ladder of success, the harder we fall. Yet every life is measured equally by God, and every heart as well.

If you pursue God's purposes and priorities, perhaps you will lose the world, but you will certainly gain your soul.

*Notes*

1. James S. Hewitt, *Illustrations Unlimited* (Wheaton, IL: Tyndale House Publishers, 1988), p. 340.
2. Margaret Nicholas, *The World's Wealthiest Losers* (London: Chancellor Press, 1997), p. 18.
3. Ibid., p. 152.
4. A. Naismith, *1200 More Notes, Quotes and Anecdotes* (London: Pickering and Inglis Ltd., 1975), p. 35.
5. Ibid.
6. Ibid.

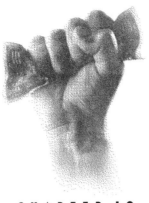

# CHAPTER 10

# BREAKING OUT OF POVERTY

*There is a sufficiency in the world for man's need but not for man's greed.*

MOHANDAS GANDHI

*If a person gets his attitude toward money straight, it will help straighten out almost every other area in his life.*

BILLY GRAHAM

It was a hot Sunday afternoon on January 8, 1956, deep in Ecuador's rain forest. Jim Elliot and four young men sat on a strip of white sand on the banks of the Curaray River, awaiting the arrival of a group of men they loved but had never met—savage, stone-age killers of the Auca Indian tribe. Just two days before, three of the tribesmen had made contact on the banks where they now sat and they had exchanged gifts.

By 4:30 that afternoon, the quiet waters of the Curaray flowed over the bodies of those five crusaders, slain by the very men they had come to win for Christ. The world called it a tragedy, but it lit fires of missionary zeal that blazed around the world. A few years later, Jim Elliot's wife, Elizabeth, along with another of the dead men's wives, Majorie Saint, returned to the place of their husbands' deaths. They had the awesome privilege of bringing with them the love of Jesus and seeing those who had murdered their husbands come to the Lord.

Years before, when he was just 20 years old, Jim Elliot had prayed and written in his journal, "Lord make my way prosperous, not that I achieve high station, but that my life may be an exhibit to the value of knowing God." God answered that prayer. Elliot never became materially wealthy or held a high position in the world's affairs, but his life was prosperous even though he died a martyr and not a millionaire. He has been dead for more than 40 years, yet his life is still a challenge and a blessing to us today. Elliot truly understood the difference between worldly riches and spiritual wealth.

# THE SPIRIT OF POVERTY

Poverty is not necessarily defined as a lack of material goods, for what is often termed poverty is relative to the time and society in which we live. Those classified as poor today may have been considered relatively wealthy just 60 or 80 years ago. The understanding of the term "poverty" in the Third World is vastly different from what is called poverty in the Western world.

Poverty is a state and a condition of always being in need—it can be spiritual, physical or both. No matter how much comes in, more always seems to go out. But poverty is more than not having; it is a spirit that is always *fearful* of not having.

By the phrase "spirit of poverty" I mean a negative spiritual condition that can be brought about by the world, the flesh or the devil. As we discussed in chapter 6, I believe the Bible supports the supposition that demonic forces can manifest themselves—i.e., influence us—in our approach to money and wealth and can be one reason why money has a hold over an individual (see Acts 19:23-27; 2 Tim. 4:10).

Again, Jesus said, "No one can serve two masters. Either he will hate the one and love the other, or he will be devoted to the one and despise the other. You cannot serve both God and Money" (Matt. 6:24). If we are serving the master of money, then we are not serving God. Can any servitude outside God's will be anything but bondage? And who is it that enslaves us? Satan. This is why I say that a person can be under the influence of a spirit of poverty.

This spirit (i.e., a condition brought on by the world, the flesh or the devil) can manifest in the wealthy and the poor, because it has to do with *the love of money*, not just with physical wealth itself. Does this mean that all poor people are enslaved by a spirit of poverty, simply because they are materially poor? Absolutely not. As we discussed, the poorest of the poor can be the most spiritually wealthy among us, if they have their lives invested in God's economy.

Does this mean that as long as we have our sights set on God's values, He does not care if we are in physical poverty? No. Though Jesus said, "The poor you will always have with you" (Mark 14:7), He was stating this as a fact of a fallen world, not as a desire of His or the Father's will. God loves us and wants us to cast all our cares upon Him. He promises that if we seek first His kingdom and His righteousness, all these things—physical needs such as food and shelter—will be given to us as well (see Matt. 6:25-34).

Jesus taught in the Sermon on the Mount that the pagans run after worldly wealth (see Matt. 6:32). They strive and pursue what God will give His children freely when they put Him first in their lives (see Matt. 6:33). He taught that the pursuit of materialism brings no peace; only worry, greed and fear.

What did Jesus mean when He said, "Blessed are the poor in spirit, for theirs is the kingdom of heaven" (Matt. 5:3)? The Greek word He used to describe "poor" here is *ptochos*, which means a person who has nothing—those who are living in abject poverty. Another Greek word that describes poverty is *penes*, which describes those who are struggling just to make ends meet. The person whom Jesus spoke of in Matthew 5:3 is the one for whom the struggle is over—there is nothing left to make ends meet, no strength to carry on. This person is destitute and no longer has the resources to do anything about it.

This does not mean that God's will is for His people to live as paupers and beggars. There is nothing very spiritual about living in a slum and seeing your family starve before your eyes. There is no bliss in such misery, and nowhere in the Bible does it teach that such poverty is a good thing. Luke 6:20 says, "Blessed are you who are poor, for yours is the kingdom of God." Jesus has a special place in His heart for the poor. Still, without Christ the poor man is no nearer the kingdom of God than the rich man. The poor may rely upon riches just as much as the wealthy: *If only I had this. If only I could get that. If only . . .*

The Old Testament use of the word "poverty" refers to those who are so poor and downtrodden that they have nowhere else to turn but to God, whereas the rich tend to rely upon themselves. For instance, when the Israelites cried out to God under the oppression of the Egyptians, God stretched out His hand in mercy and compassion. In Matthew 5, Jesus was not advocating impoverishment—far from it—but warning of the danger of riches and reliance upon one's self.

The poor in spirit is a person who has come to the place where he is so aware of his need and emptiness before God, that he is totally dependent upon Him for everything. To such a person Jesus says, "You are truly blessed for yours is the kingdom of God. You don't have it and you can't get it, but I do have it and I will give it to you" (see Matt. 5:3).

He once told His followers, "Do not be afraid, little flock, for your Father has been pleased to give you the kingdom" (Luke 12:32). He was drawing a contrast between those who rely upon self and those who rely upon God. To become a Christian means coming to an end of one's self, realizing that we do not have what it takes to make ourselves right with God. "All our righteous acts are like filthy rags" (Isa. 64:6).

Jesus told a story to illustrate this:

Two men went up to the temple to pray, one a Pharisee and the other a tax collector. The Pharisee stood up and prayed about himself, "God, I thank you that I am not like other men—robbers, evildoers, adulterers—or even like this tax collector. I fast twice a week and give a tenth of all I get."

But the tax collector stood at a distance. He would not even look up to heaven, but beat his breast and said, "God, have mercy on me, a sinner."

I tell you that this man, rather than the other, went home justified before God. For everyone who exalts himself will be humbled, and he who humbles himself will be exalted (Luke 18:10-14).

When we come to God we need to repent not only of our sins but also of trusting in ourselves. Many times the greatest hindrance to conversion is not the bad things people have done but the good things. This is what the apostle Paul meant when he said, "That I may gain Christ and be found in him, not having a righteousness of my own" (Phil. 3:8,9). He had been a highly religious and zealous Pharisee but had come to realize that all his good works and self-righteousness counted for nothing.

# LEARNING TO BREAK OUT OF POVERTY

When humankind fell in the Garden of Eden, the poverty that accompanied our expulsion was not only material but also spiritual, emotional, mental and physical. Eden was full of blessing and provision, but Adam was cast out of the garden and suddenly had to work by the sweat of his brow. Eve gave birth in great pain, sickness came, family strife occurred and eventually death was known (see Gen. 3:16-24). Worst of all, fellowship was lost with God. Instead of man being a ruler, he became a farmer and hunter and, eventually, the hunted.

We are born into this world with fingers curled and grasping, crying and clutching for what we want. Have you noticed how often we have to teach children to share? We need not send our children to "liar's school" to learn the ways of deceit, which their fallen nature and the fallen world around them will gladly teach them. Even though our minds and bodies develop, only a work of grace can remove our insatiable desires to get, to have, to keep for ourselves. This spirit of poverty must be broken if we are to enter into God's abundant provision for our lives.

Poverty means never earning enough, however much you earn; never looking pretty enough; the job never being good enough; a life never full enough. You can have a thousand relationships and still be a pauper and loser when it comes to true love. All the one-night stands and three-month romances leave you poorer than ever—and not just financially.

Advertisers make their money on this concept of consumers never having enough. *Newsweek* magazine in a survey asked those who earned less than $15,000 a year if they had achieved the American dream. Ninety-five percent said they had not. The pollsters then asked those earning $50,000 a year if *they* had achieved the American dream. A whopping 94 percent said they, too, had fallen short.

# LIBERTY THROUGH GIVING

It is not a lack of finances but a shortage of givers that so often hinders the work of God. D. L. Moody attended a meeting where a group of well-to-do Christians were asking God to remove a debt their church owed. After one of the believers finished his prayer, Moody startled the members by saying, "I do not think, if I were you, I would trouble the Lord in that matter." He went on to explain that God had already entrusted them with the resources to free the church of its debt, if they themselves would willingly give of their means.

This reminds me of the church treasurer who announced to the congregation that they needed $50,000 to repair the church roof. "I have good news and bad news," he told them. "The good news is that we have the money!" Everyone cheered. "The bad news," he continued, "is that it is in our pockets."

Show me a person not released in the grace of giving and I will show you someone who is frustrated and unfulfilled. We need to walk through life with open hands, learning to give, so we are in a place to receive. Clenched fists make it impossible for us to receive what God wants to give us. Only to the extent that we open our hands will we be in a place to receive. If we extend one finger, we can only take in return what that one finger will carry. If we open our hands fully, then we can appropriate all God wants to give us—and do through us. This is God's masterful plan for blessing and prospering our lives. This is why "it is more blessed to give than to receive" (Acts 20:35).

We need to learn that if we are at all able to give, then we cannot afford *not* to give, for God is no man's debtor. A true test of spirituality is not the size of the Bible we carry, but the stubs in our checkbooks that reveal what we have spent our money on.

## DO NOT DESPISE SMALL BEGINNINGS

Some of you are in a tight place and may be protesting, *I want to tithe and honor the Lord with my giving, but I can't afford to at present.*

Christians find themselves in this position from time to time and the standard, pithy answer is, "You cannot afford *not* to tithe." This is absolutely true, but it offers little help to someone who genuinely and sincerely wants to tithe but truly feels their present financial circumstances will not allow them.

God knows your heart's desire, so do not feel condemnation. Pray to Him about how you feel and what you want to do. Paul tells us in 2 Corinthians 9:10 that God supplies seed to the sower. Ask Him for seed to sow, and start with what you have. This may not be a full tithe, but it is a beginning, and at least you will be headed in the right direction.

Refuse to be controlled by fear and take a step of faith by putting God first with your finances. Make tithing the first requirement on your income and not the last. Do not fall into the trap of merely giving God your leftovers. Honor Him by putting Him first and He will bless you more than you can imagine.

Some people will ask me, "What should I do if my partner does not believe we should tithe?" Be sensitive and understanding with your spouse, especially if he or she is acting with genuine concern for you. It may help to offer an opportunity to speak with the pastor or church treasurer and ask any questions your spouse may have.

If your spouse is antagonistic and hostile toward your tithing, then you must seek God's wisdom for your situation. Remember, we give out of what we have and God knows your home difficulties as well as your heart's desire. Whatever you give, do it with love and sow it in faith and refuse to feel condemnation.

## DEALING WITH FINANCIAL HARDSHIP

Still others may be asking, *I tithe faithfully, so why do I know financial hardship?* It can be confusing and frustrating to hear marvelous testimonies of God's provision in other people's lives after they began tithing and putting God first in their finances. You say to yourself, *I have been doing that for years, yet I am still broke.*

Here are some possible reasons:

1. *Seasons of testing.* All Christians go through seasons of trial and testing, and tithing will not make us immune to them. God allows these times to test our faithfulness and to teach us how to trust Him. Paul learned to be content in God, no matter what the circumstances (see Phil. 4:12,13). Jesus enabled him to enjoy blessing without becoming caught up in it and to endure hardship without being cast down by it.

2. *A spiritual root.* If yours is not a season of difficulty but a lifetime of continuous struggle, then there might be a spiritual root to your problem. It could be that a spirit of poverty has come against your life and

your family. You need to seek God as to whether this may be the problem, repenting for any sins He shows you and breaking the yoke in the name of Jesus. During the reign of David, there was a crippling three-year drought. When David sought the Lord regarding this calamity, God told him the drought was on account of the sins of Saul and his blood-stained house (see 2 Sam. 21:1). Because of Saul's sin, the entire nation was under a curse. Sometimes it is necessary for us to remit not only our own sins but also the sins of our household (e.g., parents and ancestors).

3. *Legalism.* It may be that though you tithe faithfully, the act has become a legalistic discipline rather than an act of loving devotion. Perhaps your giving comes from a debt mentality and has become a mechanical function instead of a dynamic response.

4. *False teaching.* Maybe you have a wrong understanding of what God promises regarding your giving. Tithing is not going to make every Christian rich. But it provides the channel that brings the provision of God into our lives to meet our needs.

5. *Poor stewardship.* As we have seen, giving God a tithe does not mean that the rest is ours to do with as we please. Everything belongs to God and you are the steward of all that He gives to you. If you have the attitude that the tithe is God's and the rest is yours, then you are mistaken. Are you seeking God's will in how you spend the remainder of your money? Or do your spending habits contradict what tithing is all about? God is to be first and foremost in everything we do.

# THE MORE YOU LOVE, THE MORE YOU HAVE

Church life would be wonderful if the only competition among the congregation was based on who can love the others the most. My 11-year-old daughter and I have a little game we sometimes play when we say we love each other. It first started when she was five and she said that she loved me. I replied, "I love you, too."

She then responded as only a small child can, "I love you four."

I said, "I love you eight."

"I love you twenty!" she countered, and on it went.

I love those moments. You can only love by giving yourself, and you can only have love by giving it away. If you keep it, you lose it; the more you give, the more you have.

Proverbs 18:24 (*NKJV*) says, "A man who has friends must himself be friendly." You cannot make friends with clenched fists. To have friends we must first be willing to make friends. And to do that, we must be willing to *be* a friend. It was Dale Carnegie who said, "You can make more friends in two months by becoming interested in other people than you can in two years by trying to get them interested in you."

An English publication offered a prize for the best definition of a friend. Thousands of answers were received and the winner was "A friend is the one who comes in when the whole world has gone out."

A more lighthearted definition I came across says "Real friends are those who, when you have made a fool of yourself, don't think you have done a permanent job."

Proverbs 17:17 tells us "A friend loves at all times."

We must be willing to love, and this involves risk. When the late David Watson talked about this in his book *I Believe in the Church*, he quoted C. S. Lewis:

To love all is to be vulnerable. Love anything, and your heart will certainly be wrung and possibly broken. If you want to make sure of keeping it intact, you must give your heart to no one. Wrap it carefully round with hobbies and little luxuries; avoid all entanglements; lock it safe in a casket or coffin of your selfishness. But in that casket—safe, dark, motionless, airless—it will change. It will not be broken; it will become unbreakable, impenetrable, irredeemable. . . . The only place outside heaven where you can be perfectly safe from all the dangers of love is—hell.[1]

## A SERVANT'S HEART

You cannot minister to others without giving. This is why Jesus emphasized that what a person does with his or her money influences his or her life and ministry (see Luke 16:13). The gifts of the Holy Spirit are to be given away. They are not collector's items like medals or badges. They are given to us so that we can be a channel of God's blessing to others—and in so doing, exalt Jesus.

The spirit of poverty manifests itself in many people's attitudes about attending church. Many people only go for what they can get, not with the desire to give. They evaluate the service, sermon, fellowship and worship only by what they have received. The word "servant" is not high on their agenda, unless it is others who are doing the serving. You will never be effective in ministry without a servant heart.

The world judges a person's greatness by how many others serve that person. God determines greatness by how many others each person serves. F. B. Meyer put it like this: "I used to think that God's gifts were on shelves, one above the other, and the taller we grew in the Christian life the more easily we could get them. I now find that God's gifts are on shelves one beneath the other and that it is not a question of growing taller but stooping lower."

## SALVATION

One of the biggest lies the devil has spread is that if people become Christians, they will be worse off than they presently are and that they will have to give up too much for too little in return.

Consider some of the worst exchange deals in history:

Russia sold Alaska to America for just two cents an acre before Alaska's vast natural wealth was discovered.

John Pemberton created what he called a brain-nerve stimulant and sold the company that made it for $2,300. Today the company is worth $18 billion. His invention was called Coca-Cola.

Walter Hunt invented what has been classified as one of the 50 greatest inventions in the history of mankind, the safety pin. He sold his rights to the invention for just $10 to pay off a gambling debt.

In the winter of 1919, Boston Red Sox team owner Harry Frazee sold the contract of a young pitcher named George Herman "Babe" Ruth to the rival New York Yankees. The Yankees paid Frazee $125,000 in cash and advanced him a $300,000 loan, which Frazee used to finance a Broadway musical called *No, No, Nanette*. The musical was a success, but on nowhere near the scale of Babe Ruth and the Yankees. The Sultan of Swat hit an astounding 54 home runs in the 1920 season and would soon lead the Yankees to four World Series championships, setting 56 major league batting records in the process. The Yankees went on to become the most successful franchise in baseball history; the Red Sox have not won the World Series since 1918.

But the worst transaction of all is one that untold millions make without realizing their mistake until it is too late. Jesus said, "What good will it be for a man if he gains the whole world, yet forfeits his soul? Or what can a man give in exchange for his soul?" (Matt. 16:26).

What value has your eternal soul? This is what the devil prizes most; he will offer you the kingdoms of this world as long as he can have you. Your soul is also the precious commodity for which God has paid the highest price. Of all the creatures and treasures of creation, He values you most:

**THE WORST TRANSACTION OF ALL IS ONE THAT UNTOLD MILLIONS MAKE WITHOUT REALIZING THEIR MISTAKE UNTIL IT IS TOO LATE.**

> For you know that it was not with perishable things such as silver or gold that you were redeemed from the empty way of life handed down to you from your forefathers, but with the precious blood of Christ, a lamb without blemish or defect (1 Pet. 1:18,19).

# BREAKING OUT OF A POVERTY MIND-SET

At the Bible school my wife and I attended, all students received Sunday ministry postings for the entire year. After hearing of our posting for our second year in Bible college, I somewhat optimistically turned to my wife and said, "We should be well looked after with travel expenses," for our placement was a fairly large, wealthy city church. But what awaited us there I would never have thought possible.

We had to travel 120 miles, a four-hour round-trip through the center of London every Sunday. On our first Sunday at the church, the treasurer asked me how much I had paid for gasoline. I happily told him, expecting him to add that to the mileage reimbursement I was told I would receive. He proceeded to reimburse me— for the exact amount of the gas! I smiled, but underneath I was shouting, *Four hours on the road, wear and tear on the car—you can't be serious!* But he was.

Worse was to come. The following week we took a friend from college with us who had been given a ministry placement in a church a few miles from ours. Now the journey was even longer and more complicated. His church gave him £5 (about $8) for travel expenses, which he passed on to me (and with which we later bought Kentucky Fried Chicken—a rare college treat after a long day's ministry).

The following week our church treasurer found out about the other church and asked how much was given by them for my friend's traveling costs. I told the treasurer £5. What happened next I still find hard to believe. He deducted that amount from the £8 we normally received and proceeded to give me £3! Can you believe it? Three pounds for traveling four hours and 120 miles round-trip to their church. I am glad to say that such meanness did not last and we were later given the original amount (which meant we at least ate well on the way home at night). This is a prime example of the type of poverty mind-set from which we need to be set free.

The Roman prison system felt no obligation to feed its prisoners. If a prisoner starved, that was his bad fortune. The only way many prisoners stayed alive was if someone on the outside cared enough to send food or money to buy it. The apostle Paul found himself in this situation when he was imprisoned in Rome. Sadly, for a time, many of his friends forgot about him or were unaware of his circumstances. But when his plight was understood, the church at Philippi did all it could to help support him. This is the background of his letter to the Philippians.

Paul had known beatings, stonings, curses and rejection. Yet Paul's letter to the Philippians was full of joy as he responded to them in love and thankfulness. While he appreciated their gifts, he made it clear that they were not the source of his provision and joy. With his mind set firmly on Christ and God's kingdom, he knew that God would meet all his needs. Paul knew more contentment in his prison than Caesar did in his palace (see Phil. 4:10-12).

God loves us and He is for us. He does not want to bless everyone else except you. Imagine a church service with 500 present, including you. Before his sermon, the preacher says that God has given him a message that He is going to greatly bless every person in the meeting—except one. Would you feel that you were the one?

Whatever your theology or your opinion of prosperity and healing teachings, you can at least understand what the evangelist meant when he said, "If we believe God only heals and prospers a few, the devil will always tell you that you are not one of the few."

We need to learn the biblical truths affirming God's love and provision for us:

The Lord is my shepherd, I shall not want (Ps. 23:1, *NKJV*).

No weapon forged against you will prevail (Isa. 54:17).

Seek ye first the kingdom of God, and His righteousness; and all these things shall be added unto you (Matt. 6:33, *KJV*).

If God is for us, who can be against us? (Rom. 8:31).

I can do all things through Christ who strengthens me (Phil. 4:13, *NKJV*).

And my God will meet *all your needs* according to His glorious riches in Christ Jesus (Phil. 4:19, emphasis mine).

Let me clarify that it is not our positive confession that brings healing or meets our needs; it is Jesus. Positive confession—like praise and worship—places us in a position to experience what God wants to give us (see 2 Chron. 20:21-26; Acts 16:25,26). Prayer and declaration must not be turned into some kind of technique that ends up becoming little more than vain repetition. Nor will our endless quotations of Scripture bring God's blessing. Rather, blessing comes through a relationship with Him who quickens His Word to us, thus releasing our faith.

When Jesus gave His disciples what we call the Lord's Prayer, He warned them not to be like the pagans, "for they think they will be heard because of their many words" (Matt. 6:7). It is more than a little ironic that the very prayer Jesus gave to teach us not to indulge in such repetition is the prayer that many today use in exactly that way.

Jesus told us we are to pray, "Your kingdom come, your will be done, on earth as it is in heaven" (Matt. 6:10). The power and provision of His kingdom are revealed when we bring the future, not the past, into the present. We are to take hold of what God has promised and begin to taste "the goodness of the word of God and the powers of the coming age" (Heb. 6:5).

It is a characteristic of the cults, the eastern religions and the occult to turn the search for blessing into a technique, a mantra or an incantation. An amusing yet tragic illustration of this is the leader of a Christian Science church who was talking with a female member. "How is your husband today?" the leader asked.

"I'm afraid he is very ill," said the woman.

"No, no, no," corrected the leader. "You really shouldn't say that. You should say that he's under the impression that he's very ill."

The woman nodded weakly. She said, "Yes, I'll remember next time."

A week later they met again. "And how is your husband at the moment?" inquired the leader.

"Well," the woman replied, "he's under the impression that he's dead."

God wants us to be positive and full of faith (see Mark 9:23); He also wants us to be sensible and full of wisdom (see Prov. 4:5-7). Unfortunately, positive confession, faith and prayer are not always taught in a way that reveals such positive attributes. We often hear and read about amazing answers to prayer and the miracles that happen in people's lives. But we never hear about the thousands who have been left thinking that God does not love them as much because they have not received a dramatic miracle in response to their prayers.

Think positive not negative, pray health not disease, affirm the answer and not the problem, but let us not turn a divine truth into a human technique. In the wilderness temptations it was Jesus' relationship with the Father that determined how Scripture should be applied in His life—not the devil's quoting of it (see Luke 4:1-13).

We must also remember that negative confession can bring poverty of faith, giving the devil further room to work. This can prevent healing and the ability to know the joy, strength and provision of the Lord. Everything about God's kingdom is positive—life, light, joy, peace, righteousness, health, strength, love and forgiveness. Everything about Satan's kingdom is negative—death, darkness, misery, despair, sin, sickness, hatred and bitterness. The spirit of poverty feeds on negativism, fear and insecurity, which we find everywhere in today's society.

# OVERCOMING A SPIRIT FROM HELL

For you did not receive a spirit that makes you a slave again to fear, but you received the Spirit of sonship. And by him we cry "Abba, Father." The Spirit himself testifies with our spirit that we are God's children. Now if we are children, then we are heirs—heirs of God and co-heirs with Christ, if indeed we share in his sufferings in order that we may also share in his glory (Rom. 8:15-17).

Paul said there is a spirit that seeks to enslave us with fear. In Paul's time, a slave was not only bound to his master, but also most slaves lived in absolute poverty. In the Roman Empire, most slaves had nothing they could truly call their own; they were the poorest of the poor.

Jesus came to set the captives free, bringing good news to the poor and proclaiming the year of the Lord's favor (see Luke 4:18,19). This year of favor refers to the Jewish Year of Jubilee, which occurred every 50 years. All possessions and properties were returned to the rightful owners and all slaves and captives among God's people were released. Jesus came to break the yoke of hell's tyranny and restore to God's people that which was rightfully theirs. Paul said that far from being enslaved again, we should realize that we are coheirs with Christ. We share not only in His death but also in His inheritance.

This does not mean that we are to wallow in material luxury and that there will not be times of difficulty and need. Paul spoke often of hardships and trials. He wrote, "Sorrowful, yet always rejoicing, poor, yet making many rich; having nothing, yet possessing everything" (2 Cor. 6:10). You may indeed experience times of need—even great need. Yet in the midst of these times, remember what Christ has already done for you and who you are in Him:

Therefore, if anyone is in Christ, he is a new creation; the old has gone, the new has come! (2 Cor. 5:17).

You may have nothing at this moment, but you can depend upon God to meet all your needs according to His glorious riches in Christ Jesus. Why? Because you also have an inheritance in those riches—you are a coheir with Christ.

# LEARNING TO STRETCH OUT YOUR HANDS

To break out of poverty we must live in the opposite spirit. The flesh will always look for reasons not to give, telling you not to tithe and to forego sacrifice. When people do not honor the Lord with their giving, it is because their flesh is in control. So, what do you do with something that will never surrender and seeks to destroy you? You learn to put it to death. We need to crucify our flesh and stretch out our hands in surrender to God.

The Roman soldiers took Jesus' hands, which refused to grasp, and stretched them out to nail them to a cross. They opened His palms and drove great jagged nails through the bones and flesh of His wrists. They held Him up for all to see, laughing, mocking and spitting in His face. He cried out, not to curse them, but to urge, "Father, forgive them; for they know not what they do" (Luke 23:34, *KJV*).

Philippians 2:5-11 says that even though Jesus was God and equal with God, He did not consider equality something to be grasped. Jesus was willing to let go of His standing as Lord of the universe so that He could redeem mankind. Grasping hands signify a grasping spirit—we must learn to let go and open our hands to God and to others. As a result of Jesus' obedience to the Father:

> Therefore God exalted him to the highest place and gave him the name that is above every name, that at the name of Jesus every knee should bow, in heaven and on earth and under the earth, and every tongue confess that Jesus Christ is Lord, to the glory of God the Father (Phil. 2:9-11).

We see this powerful exaltation revealed in Revelation 5:13:

> Then I heard every creature in heaven and on earth and under the earth and on the sea, and all that is in them, singing: "To him who sits on the throne and to the

Lamb be praise and honor and glory and power, for ever and ever."

The angels sing, "Worthy is the Lamb, who was slain, to receive power and wealth and wisdom and strength and honor and glory and praise!" (Rev. 5:12).

The world may make one rich, the devil may give all the kingdoms of the earth, but with such riches come sorrow. The blessings of God make one rich but bring no trouble with them (see Prov. 10:22). It was Martin Luther who said, "I have held many things in my hands and lost them, but that which I have placed in God's hands I still possess."[2]

At the beginning of this chapter I mentioned a prayer Jim Elliot prayed early in his life. I conclude with another prayer he prayed, this one as he was contemplating the years ahead in serving God. He had been meditating on Hebrews 1:7, which says, "He makes . . . his servants flames of fire," when he wrote down in his journal:

Am I ignitable? God, deliver me from the dread asbestos of other things. Saturate me with the oil of Thy Spirit that I may be aflame. But flame is transient, often short lived. Canst thou bear this my soul, short life? In me dwells the Spirit of the great short lived, whose zeal for His Father's house consumed Him. He has promised baptism with the Holy Spirit and with fire. Make me Thy fuel O flame of God.

Make our lives and our finances your fuel, O flame of God!

*Notes*

1. David Watson, *I Believe in the Church* (London: Hodder and Stoughton, 1982), p. 367.

2. Robert C. Savage, *Pocket Wisdom* (Minneapolis, MN: Worldwide Publications, 1984), p. 115.

CHAPTER 11

# MONEY AND THE END OF THE AGE

*But of that day and hour no one knows, not even the angels in heaven,*
*nor the Son, but only the Father.*

MARK 13:32, NKJV

The single most significant truth of all Bible prophecy is that Jesus is coming again. Only the subject of salvation is mentioned on more occasions in Scripture. Such emphasis has long led to both comfort and confusion over what is to happen in the future.

The Church has suffered no shortage of date setters willing to predict when the Second Coming will take place. One of the most recent was in the early 1980s when a prominent space scientist, Edgar C. Whisenant, wrote a book called *88 Reasons Why the Rapture Will Be in 1988*. He figured it all out using a giant computer at NASA. The book sold 4.5 million copies. After his prediction proved wrong, Whisenant said he had accidentally miscalculated his date, and he sold thousands more copies of *The Final Shout: Rapture Report 1989.*

I like what conference speaker and writer Tony Campolo says: "I've no idea when Jesus is coming back. I'm on the welcoming committee, not the planning committee."

Even though we do not know the exact time and season of Christ's return, we are told to understand the times and the seasons of the days in which we live. We know the signs of the end times but not the end time of the signs. When you study the biblical signs, you realize that many of them relate to what will take place in the world's environments and economies. Just listen to the news and note how many of the world's problems have to do with its ecology and economies.

Many of the parables in which Jesus speaks about His Second Coming refer to or involve the use of finances. What we do with our money and our attitude toward it should be of the utmost importance to us, especially because of the days and times in which we live. Jesus said:

As it was in the days of Noah, so it will be at the coming of the Son of Man. For in the days before the flood, people were eating and drinking, marrying and giving in marriage, up to the day Noah entered the ark . . . until the flood came and took them all away (Matt. 24:37-39).

The people were so caught up in everyday living there was no mention or place for God within their lives. Sounds eerily, even alarmingly familiar, doesn't it?

# THE BEGINNING OF THE END

We are already experiencing the effects of environmental and natural destruction, all of which the Bible warns about. Some would argue that earthquakes, famines and pestilence have been with us throughout all history. During the sixth century, a plague killed an estimated 100 million people in the Middle East, Asia and Europe. In the fourteenth century, the Black Death killed 75 million people—nearly half the population of Europe. Terrible as such plagues have been, I believe what is to come will be a great deal worse.

When His disciples asked what signs would signal His return, Jesus began by telling them there would be disasters in the world—great earthquakes, wars, famines and pestilence on an unprecedented level (see Matt. 24:3-31; Luke 21:11). In Revelation 6:3-8 we read that a quarter of the earth's population will be destroyed in these cataclysmic events. And this is only the beginning of the end.

David Pawson points out in his insightful book *Explaining the Second Coming* that "the signs are clearly visible for all to see with the number of earthquakes apparently doubling every ten years."[1]

Dr. Gary Whiteford, a geography professor at the University of Brunswick, has researched every earthquake since 1900 that registered 5.8 or higher on the Richter scale. The first half of this century saw only an average of 68 big earthquakes per year. But after nuclear testing began, the average annual number increased to 127.[2]

Modern warfare has resulted in the deaths of more people in our century than in the preceding 5,000 years of history combined. Famine, too, is increasing on a frightening scale.

Since the Day of Pentecost when Peter quoted the words of the prophet Joel to explain what was taking place, we have been living in the last days (see Acts 2; Joel 2). But during this century we have witnessed an amazing acceleration of what Jesus described as "birth pangs"—signs occurring before His return. The closer a pregnant mother gets to the point of delivery, the more intense and more frequent the pains become.

I believe that not only will environmental catastrophes continue to increase, but the world will also experience a series of severe economic crises. Revelation 8:6-12 speaks of such horrific earthly disasters. Some nations will prosper as other countries experience more poverty and hunger; but there will come a time when every nation will be affected. Economic booms will turn to busts as financial shock waves circle the world, with the major financial markets becoming increasingly dependent upon each other. Ecological devastation and economic nightmares will cause widespread alarm and panic. In such a mood, people will look for a savior to avert annihilation. Jesus warned His disciples to be on the watch and not to be taken in by the false messiahs and prophets who will appear (see Matt. 24:11).

As we discussed in chapter 4, Keynesian economics emphasizes that the government has the ability to manage and guide the life of a society. This economic philosophy of "government as savior" has put the nations of the world in the position where they must come together under a form of international control. The beginnings of this can be seen in the coming together of the European Union (EU), in which the major nations of Europe are coalescing under one currency, the Eurodollar. NATO's unprecedented role in Kosovo—where 19 nations worked together to quell ethnic and national conflict—is another sign of such supracooperation among nations. While such international cooperation is not always a bad thing in and of itself, these world events point to the biblical signs of the last days.

# THE DAY THE DOLLAR DIES

In 1973, Willard Cantelon published his best-selling book *The Day the Dollar Dies*. Through the prophetic writings of the Bible and a study of the world's financial activities, Cantelon proclaimed that in the years ahead we will see unprecedented collapse and change in the world's money markets and economies. He described how even the mighty American dollar will finally collapse and how financial ruin will result.

In 1939, Cantelon began speaking about the new-world money system that would be established in the future. He quoted the apostle John to help depict the world events that will take place, leading to a one-world government and a universal monetary system:

**THE STAGE IS SET FOR A CHARISMATIC INDIVIDUAL TO RISE TO POWER—SOMEONE WHO CLAIMS TO BE ABLE TO RESOLVE THE ECONOMIC CHAOS AND CALAMITY PERVADING OUR PLANET.**

> When the Lamb opened the fourth seal, I heard the voice of the fourth living creature say, "Come!" I looked, and there before me was a pale horse! Its rider was named Death, and Hades was following close behind him. They were given power over

a fourth of the earth to kill by sword, famine and plague, and by the wild beasts of the earth (Rev. 6:7,8).

The stage is now set for a charismatic individual to rise to power—someone who claims to be able to resolve the chaos and calamity pervading our planet. This person will rule like a dictator as the troubles coming on the earth reach a climax known as the Great Tribulation (see Rev. 7:14). This ruler was called the antichrist by John (see 1 John 2:18). Note that in the Greek language *anti* means "instead of"—a substitute rather than an antagonist. In 2 Thessalonians 2:3,4, Paul talked about a "man of lawlessness" who would oppose and exalt himself over everything and even set himself up in the Temple, proclaiming himself to be God. But he is doomed to destruction.

Such is the judgment and devastation described in Revelation chapters 6–12. In chapter 13 this dictator is described as a "beast" (see v. 1), as is his coconspirator, the false prophet who will deceive the inhabitants of the earth (see v. 14). I believe that together they will establish a totalitarian regime under which only those who submit to their authority—by being branded with their mark—will be able to buy and sell goods. The mark will be the number 666. The number's meaning will be obvious when that time comes, but six is the Hebrew number of humanity, always falling short of the divine perfection of the number seven.

# NUCLEAR HOLOCAUST

In the late 1970s God began bringing groups of Christian leaders together to prepare for a mass exodus of Jews from Soviet Russia. These Christians came together with the conviction that this was the return from the north that Jeremiah said would take place in the last days (see Jer. 23:7,8). Only one nation north of Israel had any sizable number of Jews: the Soviet Union with 2.1 million Jewish residents. This type of mass exodus seemed impossible at the time. The Soviet Union was at the peak of its military power and world influence. Jews who applied for extradition were harassed and imprisoned. But God had already begun to make a way.

In 1979, the Soviet grain harvests were disastrous; the Union could not feed itself. Half of its hard currency went toward food imports. The death of Konstantin Chernenko, short-lived president of the USSR, cleared the way in 1985 for the meteoric rise of the lesser-known Mikhail Gorbachev. At that time, less than 100 Jews a month were allowed to emigrate; more than 360,000 who dared to apply had been refused.

In the 1980s, teams of intercessors traveled to the major Jewish population centers in the Soviet Union. In each respective city, the prayer warriors encircled at least one of the many giant statues of Lenin, praying and proclaiming that this idol would fall. One group went to the Moscow River beside the Kremlin, and led by God, took a Bible marked with passages of judgment, tied it to a large stone and threw it through the thin ice covering the river. "Thus the Soviet Union shall sink and not rise from the catastrophe that the Lord will bring upon her," they declared in the name of the Lord. Just four months later came an event that rocked the Soviet Union and shook the world: the explosion at the Chernobyl nuclear reactor in the Ukraine.

The winter 1991 issue of the *University of Pacific Review* offers a chilling description of what went wrong in the 1986 Chernobyl disaster:

> There were two electrical engineers in the control room
> that night, and the best thing that could be said for what

they were doing is they were "playing around" with the machine. They were performing what the Soviets later described as an unauthorized experiment. They were trying to see how long a turbine would "freewheel" when they took the power off. Taking the power off that kind of nuclear reactor is a dangerous thing to do, because these reactors are very unstable in their lower ranges. In order to get the reactor down to that kind of power, where they could perform the test they had in mind, they had to manually override six separate computer-driven systems. One by one the computers would come up and say, "Stop! Dangerous! Go no further!" and one by one they shut off the alarms and kept going.[3]

The reactor exploded with devastating effect, emitting as much long-term radiation into the world's air, topsoil and water as all the bombs that had ever been exploded in nuclear tests—40 times the energy of the two atom bombs dropped on Japan in World War II.

The immediate area surrounding the Chernobyl facility became a death zone, or Forbidden Zone. Only a few elderly residents stayed, refusing to leave as hundreds of thousands were later evacuated. Local and regional Communist party officials attempted to cover up what was happening, sending their children away while ordering others to march in May Day celebrations—even as a lethal radioactive cloud hung over the region. The firemen and soldiers first drafted to control the fire did so without any protective clothing. All are now dead, having suffered terribly. I have seen the video testimony of some of those firemen before they died; their suffering and heartbreak were overwhelming.

It was only when the cloud rained down contamination on Poland and the Scandinavian countries that the story began to leak out. When the full truth became known, the communist regime was exposed as callous and devious. The Soviet Union's own people lost faith and became more critical of the Communist system. All these events were paving the way for the eventual collapse of the Union, which occurred just a few years later.

The full consequences of the Chernobyl disaster are only just now being felt. The shattered reactor was encased in a concrete tomb that is beginning to disintegrate because of the nuclear activity inside. A good friend of mine who visited the area a few years ago told me how he was able to tear off a handful of concrete from the shell. If the unstable reactor were to leak, the potential catastrophe could be worse than the original disaster. Huge clouds of radioactive dust could explode into the atmosphere if the casing were to give way. This is not the only danger as Chernobyl still has three remaining active nuclear reactors. The world is yet to hear the last of Chernobyl.

Just a few months after the explosion an amazing report appeared in many of the world's newspapers, including *The New York Times*. On the front page of the July 26, 1986 edition, a dispatch from Moscow read:

> A prominent Russian writer recently produced a tattered old Bible and with a practiced hand turned to Revelation. "Listen," he said, "this is incredible: 'The third angel sounded his trumpet, and a great star, blazing like a torch, fell from the sky on a third of the rivers and on the springs of water—the name of the star is Wormwood. A third of the waters turned bitter, and many people died from the waters that had become bitter'" (Rev. 8:10,11).

Using a dictionary he showed the Ukrainian meaning for wormwood, which is a bitter herb used as a tonic in rural Russia. The Ukrainian word: "chernobyl."

# THE VISION

In his book *The Vision*, Teen Challenge founder David Wilkerson talks about two visions he has had in his lifetime. The first occurred in 1958, which led to the ministry of Teen Challenge. The second vision came to him in the summer of 1973, revealing details of five calamities that would come upon the earth. Wilkerson writes:

> While I was in prayer one night these visions of world calamities came over me with such impact that I could do nothing but kneel, transfixed, and take it all in. At first I did not want to believe what I saw and heard. The message of the vision was too frightening, too apocalyptic, too discomforting to my materialistic mind. But the vision came back to me night after night. I couldn't shake it off.[4]

The first part of the vision he calls "Economic Confusion." The opening words: "A crash is coming." He clearly saw that "not only is the American dollar headed for deep trouble, but so are all other world currencies." He goes on to say, "Those who don't prepare are going to get hurt. People who spend recklessly and buy unneeded material things will suffer the most."

Wilkerson continues:

> There will develop a call for revamping all world monetary systems into one uniform system. I believe a revived Roman Empire will eventually become the power base for a super world leader who will arise to restore economic order. He will no doubt institute a worldwide "walking credit card" system. Invisible numbers will be

implanted on the forehead and forearm. This mark would be required by all and no one could buy or sell without this invisibly tattooed number.[5]

I believe that economic ruin is indeed coming. The world's money markets will be in a sudden free fall. Currencies will lose their value overnight. Everything man prides himself on will be shaken and destroyed.

Into this carnage a new world order, money system and leader will arise:

> And he was given authority over every tribe, people, language and nation. He also forced everyone, small and great, rich and poor, free and slave, to receive a mark on his right hand or on his forehead, so that no one could buy or sell unless he had the mark, which is the name of the beast or the number of his name (Rev. 13:7,16,17).

Dr. Henry Spaak, former secretary general of NATO once said, "What we want is a man of sufficient stature to hold the allegiances of all the people and to lift us out of the economic morass into which we are sinking. Send us such a man, and be he god or devil, we will receive him."

Now, nearly 30 years later, the technological explosion means that what was unthinkable in 1973, when Wilkerson wrote his book, is now possible. Scientific and technological knowledge is reckoned to be doubling every 14 months. We live in a global village where all the major economies are linked together. The signs are there for all to see. In the light of this, what bearing should it have on us regarding our finances for the present and the future?

# THE LAST CHAPTER IS YET TO BE WRITTEN

When these things begin to take place, stand up and lift
up your heads, because your redemption is drawing near
(Luke 21:28).

What then should be our response to the uncertainties now facing us?

1. We must not panic. God is in full control. Terrible confusion and heartache have been caused by those who have set dates and given detailed predictions for the end of the age and the Second Coming. Even the books and sources I have quoted should only be seen as helpful in giving the big picture and not as a complete or definitive picture.
2. We should invest our lives and possessions wisely, being more concerned with what God would have us do than with what our financial advisor might suggest.
3. Beware of going into debt for things you do not need.
4. Do not allow yourself to become sucked into the world's obsession with materialism and control (e.g., obsessions with money markets and financial institutions).
5. More than ever before, now is the time to be generous in supporting the work of missions to reach the lost.
6. If we do not trust and honor God with our money now, we will have nothing to draw upon and sustain us in the future.
7. Finally, we will all have to stand before God and give an account of what we have done. Those who have reject-

ed God's love and salvation through Jesus will pay the ultimate penalty for their sins, eternally suffering the consequences of being separated from God. Those who have acknowledged Jesus as Savior and Lord will give account of how they lived and what they have done with what has been entrusted to them (see 2 Cor. 5:10).

What will Jesus say about you? My prayer and hope is that He will say, "Well done, good and faithful servant! You have been faithful with a few things; I will put you in charge of many things. Come and share your master's happiness" (Matt. 25:23).

Or will He say, "You wicked, lazy servant!" (Matt. 25:26)?

There is a story told about a rich and covetous man who called on his rabbi for advice concerning his unhappiness of heart and mind. The rabbi listened patiently. Then, calling the miser to the window, he said, "Tell me, what do you see there through the window?"

Looking down into the street, the unhappy man replied, "I see men, women and little children."

"Now come with me," said the rabbi, as he led his visitor across the room to a large mirror. "What do you see in there?"

Glaring at his own unhappy face, the rich man hesitated for a moment and then replied, "I see myself."

"Exactly," said the rabbi. "There is glass in the mirror and in the window; but as soon as you put *silver* behind the glass, you fail to see others and see only yourself."

It was Sir Winston Churchill, Britain's wartime prime minister, who said, "You make a living by what you get, but you only make a life by what you give." Biblical giving is far more than what we do with a proportion of our money. It is the positioning of one's whole self and life to be a channel of God's grace into this world.

If you dream of becoming rich only by getting, then you will never have enough. When you become a giver, you are saying you have enough to let some go, which means you are truly rich.

*Notes*
1. David Watson, *I Believe in the Church* (London: Hodder and Stoughton, 1982), p. 367.
2. Robert C. Savage, *Pocket Wisdom* (Minneapolis, MN: Worldwide Publications, 1984), p. 115.
3. Tim Rice, "Nukes and Quakes: A Dangerous Coincidence?" *Sojourners Magazine* (January 1993), pp. 32, 33.
4. David Wilkerson, *The Vision* (New York: Fleming Revell, 1980).
5. Ibid.

# RECOMMENDED READING

Barclay, William. *Revelation*. London: St. Andrews Press, 1959.

Breese, Dave. *Seven Men Who Rule the World from Their Graves*. Chicago: Moody Press, 1990.

Cantelon, Willard. *The Day the Dollar Dies*. New Jersey: Logos International, 1973.

Estabrooks, Paul. *Secrets to Spiritual Success*. London: Sovereign World, 1998.

Foster, Richard. *Money, Sex and Power*. London: Hodder and Stoughton, 1985.

Hayford, Jack. *The Key to Everything*. Waco, TX: Word Books, 1993.

Hinn, Benny. *The Biblical Road to Blessing*. Nashville: Thomas Nelson Publishers.

Jones, Martyn Lloyd. *Studies in the Sermon on the Mount*. London: InterVarsity Press, 1960.

Kendall, R. T. *Tithing*. London: Hodder and Stoughton, 1982.

Olford, Stephen. *The Grace of Giving*. Grand Rapids, MI: Zondervan Publishing House, 1972.

Rees, Tom. *Money Talks*. London: Billing and Sons, 1963.

Scheller, Gustav. *Operation Exodus*. London: Sovereign World, 1998.